OPERATION THUNDERBOLT

Operation Thunderbolt
The Nazi warships' escape 1942

by

Peter G. Cooksley

ROBERT HALE · LONDON

© *Peter G. Cooksley 1981*
First published in Great Britain 1981

ISBN 0 7091 9435 8

Robert Hale Limited
Clerkenwell House
Clerkenwell Green
London EC1R 0HT

Photoset by Rowland Phototypesetting Limited
Printed in Great Britain by
St Edmundsbury Press, Bury St Edmunds, Suffolk
Bound by Weatherby Woolnough Ltd, Northants

Contents

"Nowadays, people are inclined to be cynical about heroism or embarrassed by it . . .

"One of the most dangerous fashions of our own time is the tendency to belittle human beings and to reduce them to the lowest common denominator of greed and self-interest and to deny the element of altruism and even heroism in the human character."

Dr Robert Runcie,
Archbishop of Canterbury

Illustrations

Maps and drawing in the text

Picture credits

Only a few of the photographs come from the author's collection, the bulk having been drawn from the files of the Imperial War Museum, and grateful acknowledgement is made for permission to reproduce them and for the time and trouble taken by the staff at Lambeth in assisting in the choice of suitable prints.

Sincere thanks are also due to Bruce Robertson, with whom it is always a pleasure to work, for lending photographs from his own collection as well as making available some additional material via the archives of Squadron Leader M. Williamson.

Acknowledgements

Thanks for assistance received in gathering information for this work are most gratefully offered to the following persons and facilities; their enthusiasm and knowledge greatly lightened the task of preliminary research and have cleared up several questions that arose later in the pursuit of accuracy.

Chaz Bowyer

D. T. Bradley, Assistant Keeper of the Library, National Maritime Museum

Mr and Mrs J. Brooker

Eric C. Bull of the Kent Defence Research Group

Lieutenant-Commander L. A. Cox RN (Retd) of the Fleet Air Arm Museum, Yeovilton

John A. Guy, Dover Branch Secretary of the Kent Defence Research Group

Leslie Jessop

John Macdonald

R. W. Phillips of the Meteorological Office

Public Records Office, Kew

Bruce Robertson

Miss M. W. Thirkettle of the Naval Historical Branch, MoD

Harry Woodman

Finally, I am sincerely obliged to Dr Robert Runcie, Archbishop of Canterbury, for his kindness in allowing me to quote from his address delivered at Biggin Hill on 21st September 1980.

Preface

National characteristics are no longer in fashion—a strange state of affairs this, since with all our knowledge of diet, climate and geography, each of which must leave their mark on the genetic engineering of a race long subject to them, it is generally pretended that racial differences do not exist and that all mankind in every land is a sad, grey, uniform and infinitely boring carbon copy of its brother.

However justified this idea (which Plato might have equated with his 'noble lie') may be, the fact remains unchanged that various races do have differing desires, joys, hopes and tastes, and one of the stranger ones that mark the Anglo-Saxon and his transatlantic cousin is a tendency to idealize his failures, many of them military and a few civil, and to remember them as amounting almost to success, perhaps because achievements, even negative ones, made under stress and adversity give a transitory feeling of superiority to those who see it all from a safe distance in time.

Whatever the reason for this may be, a glance at history proves it to be true, and even a slight knowledge of the subject throws up such examples as Harold Godwinson's hopeless fight at Senlac, Colonel Jim Bowie's last stand at the Alamo, the plight of the prisoners in the Black Hole of Calcutta, the Light Brigade's Charge at Balaclava, the near-failure of the Battle of Britain, Pearl Harbour, Arnhem . . . The list grows long already, even without the addition of gallant failures in the field of exploration, Captain Scott at the South Pole, Malory's disappearance on Everest: there are many here too, and one wonders how long the list will be before it is lengthened by events in our own time, the abortive American attempt to rescue the hostages in Iran being a prime candidate.

Another is the failure to prevent the escape up the English Channel of the Nazi warships in 1942, the 'Operation Thunderbolt' of this book. But in the re-telling of this story an attempt has been made to strip away as much as possible of the so-called 'glamour' of the situation. The accumulation of this is a natural process of time since even before the Norse Sagas which sang in expansive terms of some of the bloodiest encounters.

There will be a few who would argue that only in this way can something be salvaged from failures and their memory turned to profit by thinking men; anything else means the final condemnation of the memory of actions such as this to a mere excuse for ceremonial—which must thereby become hollow and meaningless, while the squandering of skill, tenacity, human endeavour and material ability becomes no more than a hideous charade, so that the human lives, surviving and extinguished, that were involved need never have existed.

London, 1981   PETER G. COOKSLEY

1

Salmon and Gluckstein

"OK sir?"

"OK Jess!" With the ritual slap of the hand on the fuselage of the Spitfire, Sergeant Jessop slid off the wing. He gathered his greatcoat more closely about himself as he turned to watch the Kenley Station-Commander take off. The general air of misery was even reflected in the February weather, for it was still bitterly cold, and the grey clouds which hung over the little Surrey RAF Station and the patches of unmelted snow that lay about did nothing to improve the situation. Even the normally cheerful sergeant was unable to suppress a pang of envy at the sight of the two fighters lifting from the frozen grass; at least for the two occupants there was to be a short time seeking excitement in the air over France.

The first pilot was Group-Captain F. V. Beamish DSO, DFC, AFC, who commanded the fighter base that was the centre of the Spitfire Wing made up of the Australian 452 Squadron, New Zealand's 485 and No 602 from Glasgow. There were few who would have disagreed with this choice of Group-Captain, big, genial and friendly so that a superb rapport existed between him and his men at all levels, not forgetting the ebullient sergeant, his personal fitter; it was generally agreed that Victor Beamish was the epitome of the phrase 'officer and gentleman'.

With him as the two Spitfires climbed into the leaden sky at exactly 10.10 a.m. was Wing-Commander R.F. Boyd DFC, another survivor of the Battle of Britain. It was his job to protect—as far as possible—his superior, who, more rightly, was expected 'to fly a desk' had it not been for the special dispensation of No 11 Group's commander, Air Vice-Marshal Trafford Leigh-Mallory, the controversial officer destined to become AOC-in-C of Fighter Command nine months later, who was at present indulging his belief that his staff officers should keep alive the killer instinct.

As the pair of fighters gained height before setting course for Dungeness, where they were to cross the coast, the weather seemed temporarily more hopeful, but this was hidden from those on the ground who went about their tasks, both service and civilian, with a strange air of foreboding.

Waiting to begin their chilly journeys to London at the little railway stations of Whyteleafe and Upper Warlingham, which lay just down the road from Kenley aerodrome, late business-men pondered their four-page newspapers. Despite the un-written law that civilian morale must be kept up at all costs, most of the papers ran headlines declaring the Japanese claim that Singapore had fallen and that the garrison of thirty thou-sand was surrounded, while for good measure a few column-inches announced that the basic petrol ration for private motor-ists was to be reduced by a further sixth; with an increase of 2s 6d (12½p) in the price of beer per barrel, even the cost of a drink was likely to be increased. As they stamped their feet to keep the circulation going, the little knots of men tried not to depress each other further by pointing out how resolutely the gods of war seemed set against the Allies at the moment, for by then it was known by the better-informed few that, only ten days before, the Nazi radio had announced in gloating tones that Wing-Commander Stanford Tuck had been shot down and taken prisoner outside Boulogne.

On a course of 170 degrees and at an altitude of no more than 50 feet, Beamish and Boyd were shortly afterwards roaring over the Walland Marsh and across the Dover Strait, keeping their eyes hopefully open for trouble.

In sight of the coast at Le Touquet they were not long in finding it in the shape of a couple of Messerschmitt 109Fs flying south-west at 500 feet altitude. With an exchange of waves through the rain-lashed perspex of their canopies, the two pilots pushed their boost to 9 pounds at 2,850 revs and gave chase without seeming to gain on the enemy, who appeared to have overlooked their pursuers.

The four machines quickly lost height as the Messerschmitts made for the direction of Boulogne, and almost at once the

Spitfires were in the midst of a group of Nazi fighters, with Beamish at a slightly greater height than his companion. It was exactly 10.42 a.m. when the two saw below them a veritable armada of vessels, including at least two battle-cruisers with high, tripod mast, three destroyers and about a dozen E-boats, and the gunners on the entire fleet immediately sent up a curtain of fire. In the spirit of fighting back no matter what the odds, the Wing-Commander flung his machine into a shallow dive from 450 feet straight at the rearmost E-boat and gave it a six-second burst of fire before turning away to make room for an attack by Victor Beamish. As he did so, he thought that the vessel appeared to be burning. The fresh attack made sure of this, and the boat was left spewing smoke for 300 yards across the sea and listing so heavily that it seemed to be sinking.

The enemy fleet was sailing in line ahead with, to seaward, an inner screen of destroyers flanked in turn by a vic formation of E-boats, each section consisting of a line of four vessels. It was obvious from the size and arrangement of the ships that this was no ordinary convoy but the long-awaited break-out of the Nazi squadron from Brest, taking place not (as had long been expected by British authority) during the hours of darkness but in broad daylight.

Although identification was by no means positive, it had long been argued since that in the circumstances the Group-Captain would have been justified in disobeying orders about radio silence and throwing the switch, to yell into his microphone the code-word, 'Fuller', that would have alerted those responsible for the immediate taking of counter-measures. However, perhaps the most likely explanation is not any reluctance to break radio silence, which might have been justified in the light of the likelihood of the Spitfires being shot down, but that advanced in the official history by Captain Stephen Roskill who states that, with the fighters flying at nearly sea-level, a wireless message could not have got through, so that it was not until they landed at 11.09 a.m. that any report was made.

What the pair seem not to have realized was that they were not the only fighters in the area: there were two more Spitfires from 91 Squadron at Hawkinge sent specifically to investigate the rotating plots with the unusually large 'blip' that Biggin Hill's radar was showing moving up the Channel at a speed of which a normal convoy was incapable. The 91 Squadron machines were flown by Squadron-Leader R.W. Oxspring, a very experienced officer who had achieved a steadily rising score of 'kills' since the summer of two years before when he had flown as a Pilot Officer with No 66 Squadron. On this wet Thursday morning he was accompanied by Sergeant Beaumont.

At almost the same moment as the two from Kenley found themselves over the fleet, the second pair were diving out of clouds at about 1,500 feet, less than 20 miles off the Le Touquet coast, only to be greeted in their turn by a hail of fire. This unfriendly greeting was no guarantee that the vessels were hostile, since in certain RAF circles the Royal Navy had a reputation for shooting at anything that flew. At almost the same moment a gaggle of Nazi fighters were seen to be bearing down on them, so, deciding that attack was the best form of defence, the pair from 91 Squadron closed in to deal with the nearer two. As the range closed and identification was simpler through the wet hoods, they realized that these were in fact a couple of Spitfires, those from Kenley, so the newcomers, now convinced that the fleet was in truth Nazi, made for home with all speed. On the way Bob Oxpring shouted over the radio not the galvanizing code-word (only those more senior than himself knew what it was) but a simple estimate of the position, size and content of the fleet, prefixed by his call-sign, before streaking for base with all speed, hoping to remain alive long enough to raise the alarm properly at Hawkinge.

The three ships at the centre of this unexpected activity were the *Scharnhorst*, *Gneisenau* and *Prinz Eugen*, all of which, despite promising careers at the outbreak of war, had long been resident at Brest. There, over the immediately previous two months, they had attracted the attention of the RAF to such an extent that the effort to build up the bombing-campaign against Nazi industry was slowed considerably, and over this period no less than 1,161 missions had been mounted against the docks and surrounding areas of north-west France that had first been made a marine arsenal by Richelieu three hundred years earlier.

According to the Navy of Nazi Germany, both the *Scharnhorst* and her sister ship the *Gneisenau* were battle-ships, but in the light of the fact that they had a turn of speed superior to that of their British counterparts, the Royal Navy always referred to them as 'battle-cruisers'. The *Renown* and *Repulse* were the only British capital ships capable of matching the Nazi battle-cruisers in speed and outclassing them in firepower, since 'Salmon and Gluckstein', as they were to be later humorously named by the RAF, were the innovators of a new warship concept that had been achieved by the sacrifice of armament to gain speed, although the armour was not reduced and conformed to the ideas of the period. The heaviest armament consisted of nine 11-inch guns supported by a dozen 5·9-inch, fourteen of 4·1-inch calibre and sixteen of 37 millimetres, plus originally eight 20-millimetre anti-aircraft guns, but plans were afoot to re-equipment both vessels with six 15-inch guns in three turrets containing two each.

Scharnhorst had been launched on 30th October 1936 and was completed by Marinewerft, Wilhelmshaven, on 7th January three years later. At first she had a straight stem, whereon her pale blue shield with its silver bend made a brave showing; at a later date, just before the outbreak of war, these cruiser stems were modified both on this vessel and on *Gneisenau* in favour of clipper bows and a slightly increased forward sheer, to improve the sea-keeping qualities. At the same time, in order to keep smoke from the gunnery equipment, both vessels had a cowl added to the funnel.

Gneisenau was launched by Deutsche Werke at Kiel on 8th December 1936 and, with a complement of 1,840, a displacement of 31,800 tons (32,310 tonnes) and a length of 742 feet, was the same as her sister ship. Both had a radius of action of 10,000 miles at 17 knots and a maximum speed of 31·5 knots.

Despite the limitations imposed by the Treaty of Versailles, which demanded a maximum displacement of 10,000 tons for cruisers, the degree to which this was ignored by the 'Hipper'-class vessels may be judged by the *Prinz Eugen*, which was no less than 12,750 tons. The builder was Germania Werft of Kiel, and it was from there that she was launched on 22nd August 1938; the sea-trials which followed completion indicated a speed of 32 knots and a range of 5,500 miles at 18 knots. Main armament consisted of eight 8-inch guns with a dozen of 4·1-inch calibre plus twelve 37-millimetre and eight 20-millimetre anti-aircraft guns. The complement was sixteen hundred officers and men, and like the battle-cruisers she was fitted with funnel cowls and clipper bows in 1941-2, features in common with other major Nazi surface vessels—which tended to make identification difficult, although with a length of only 654 feet the 'Hipper' class was the smaller.

The existence of the three major vessels in the drama taking place in the English Channel on 12th February 1942 had really begun eight years before, when the two battle-cruisers were laid down and when the offer was made to Great Britain of a new and permanent agreement to replace the provisions of the now renounced Treaty—Nazi Germany now felt sufficiently confident to renounce it. This agreement stated that Germany expected to have a navy at 35-per-cent strength-ration of that of the British Isles, and the British Government had little alternative than to agree, after seeking Admiralty advice. The resultant new tonnage was distributed between the three *Deutschlands*—in fact the ship of that name, later to become the *Lutzow*, the *Graf Spee*, scuttled after the Battle of the River Plate, and the *Admiral Scheer*, and two vessels termed at the time "a pair of *Scharnhorsts*".

British thinking behind all this was to delay as long as possible the increasing German parity, since it was confidently believed that there would be no major European war until 1940, although Hitler's personal thinking was indicated as putting this date forward a further three or four years.

Meanwhile the Royal Navy enjoyed the position of being not only the oldest navy in continuous existence but also the strongest in the world, a condition that was to continue until a short time before the end of World War II, when its numerical strength was exceeded by that of the United States. However, this in no way reduced the reputation of the Royal Navy, which was second to none and was based so strongly on technical skill, seamanship and resource that Britain provided the model for nearly every other navy in the world.

The justification of this state of affairs was based firmly on two factors. First of these was the unbroken experience of British marine architects, who had amassed a vast experience quite unrivalled anywhere else, as might be expected from an island race who had made the sea their own from the days of the Channel Rovers in early Tudor times. That this was geographic necessity as much as anything else was of course true, since the position of these islands on the edge of a largely hostile continent meant that the defence of their sea-lanes was a simple matter of life and death. This in turn meant that the only way to deal with the ever-present threat was to have a large number of vessels that could be employed to cover the complete length of the not-inconsiderable coastline. Thus the design emphasis had always been not only on ships capable of operating alone or in small numbers but likewise on comparatively small, fast vessels as heavily armed as was compatible with mobility, for the second tenet had always been that, since no enemy could attack in over-many positions at any one time, there were always reinforcements not far off, although the unwritten law existed that this was never to be taken as a certainty. British ship-design had, therefore, for centuries been based on these factors, none of which allowed any margin for error.

The second major principle giving British naval superiority was that the largest mercantile navy in the world was British so that a large source of manpower existed with a skill and knowledge quite unrivalled, while the demands of the country's position, already outlined, meant that these men were adaptable, highly trained and controlled under all conditions, and history ensured that morale was always of the highest order. Much the same may also be said of the British ship-building industry which had to turn these demands and influences into concrete terms.

In some measure, the position with regard to the navies of Europe in general and Germany in particular was very much the reverse of the British situation, for the maintenance of their maritime supply-routes never assumed the qualities of a struggle for survival while overland communications existed, and the shorter coastlines could never produce the quantity of skilled men that an island must do.

It naturally followed that the vessels of the Royal Navy tended to be smaller and less highly specialized than the warships conceived on grandiose scale in Germany. The only way of restricting Germany had turned out after the end of the First World war to be international legislation, by such means as the now-moribund Treaty of Versailles. The result was that Nazi Germany was now producing battle-cruisers in a tonnage class in excess of the much-vaunted Dreadnought battleships of

1916 exactly twenty years later, despite attempts to frustrate the production of war weapons after 1918, although the armament was lighter, consisting of 11-inch as opposed to 15-inch guns as the main firepower.

After the outbreak of war in 1939, the new *Scharnhorst* and *Gneisenau* at once began to cause as much anxiety as had their earlier namesakes in the previous conflict until they were sent to the bottom off the Falkland Islands. Hitler's vessels were at first detailed to operate jointly, and together they achieved considerable success. Perhaps the best-known of these early actions was that involving the armed merchant cruiser *Rawalpindi* during the Norwegian campaign, which the *Scharnhorst* finally sank on 23rd November 1939.

Both battle-cruisers were still operating together when, on 9th April the following year, they encountered a force consisting of HMS *Renown* and nine destroyers while on the way to their patrol-stations in connection with the same theatre of war. Under conditions of combined heavy snow showers and squalls, fire was opened at 4.05 a.m. at 9 miles range, despite the very heavy seas which were breaking over the vessels. Although these conditions made little difference to the *Scharnhorst*, which had only to use her after-guns, they had serious consequences for *Renown*, the sights of her guns being on occasion partly obscured by snow and freezing spray. Captain Simeon claimed two hits by 11-inch shells, but little damage was done as both failed to explode. The entire engagement lasted no more than thirty minutes, but during this time the action was confined to the capital ships as the weather continued to deteriorate, so that the destroyers were at first unable to take part in the exchange of fire and later found it impossible to keep up.

Although the damage to her sister ship was slight, *Gneisenau* was considerably less lucky, since the first hit put her main armament-control out of action. Hardly had this happened than the Royal Navy demonstrated that they had now found the target's range by scoring a second hit with a 15-inch shell that knocked out the battle-cruiser's forward turret. During this exchange *Renown* also took some punishment in the form of two hits from the Nazi vessels, but the damage was slight. As if to redress the balance, *Gneisenau* then took a third 15-inch shell, but only limited hurt was inflicted by this one.

At about 5 a.m. the weather was still deteriorating, but when *Gneisenau* took advantage of a sudden squall to break off the engagement, *Renown* immediately gave chase. To have any hope of catching her quarry, it was necessary to make all possible speed, and the battleship managed to reach a maximum of 29 knots that allowed a final glimpse of the Nazi, but no further fire was exchanged, and it must be conceded that the final victor on this occasion was the weather.

Seven months were to elapse before the next major engagement involving the two battle-cruisers took place in the fateful month of June 1940. Both were participating in 'Operation Juno' which was directed at the British evacuation transports operating west of Harstad, Captain Hoffmann being in charge of the *Scharnhorst* while Captain Netzbandt was on the bridge of *Gneisenau*. With these two vessels was one of the *Prinz Eugen*'s sister ships, the *Admiral Hipper*, while the fleet was augmented by the destroyers *Karl Galster*, *Hans Lody*, *Erich Steinbrinck* and *Hermann Schömann*.

The first victories of this force took place on 5th June with the sinking of the tanker *Oil Pioneer*, and this was quickly joined by the *Orama*, an empty troopship and the trawler *Juniper*. But the chief prize had yet to be found.

This took the form of the aircraft-carrier *Glorious*, in the area in connection with the RAF squadrons operating against the Nazi occupation of Norway. The carrier had already brought eighteen pilots and their machines from Scapa Flow in April and had returned with replacement fighters scheduled for delivery to Narvik in mid May. Now, less than a month later, she was acting as an evacuation vessel from this same port, and Hawker Hurricanes of No 46 Squadron and Gloster Gladiators of No 263 Squadron were flown on and picketed down on the deck. Captain D'Oyly-Hughes put to sea on 7th June but the following day encountered the two Nazi battle-cruisers which quickly sank the carrier, sending down with her almost the entire strength of both squadrons. There were only forty-three survivors including but two of the Hurricane pilots. All ten of those attached to the Gladiator Squadron were lost.

In the waters crowded by the collapse of the British Norwegian campaign it was not difficult for the Nazi vessels to find further victims, and these included the destroyers *Acasta* (Commander Glasford) and *Ardent* (Lieutenant-Commander Barker), although the former ship claimed a torpedo hit on *Scharnhorst* before her own end came. Only three survivors were found and taken from the sea following this action.

HMS *Renown* was scheduled to have a second brush with the *Scharnhorst* a little after this, when, in company with *Rodney* and a number of destroyers, she was detailed to cover the movements of the aircraft-carrier *Ark Royal*. This took the form of a raid by the Home Fleet on Trondheim, and the action included a strike by fifteen Blackburn Skua dive-bombers. The date was 13th June, and they were dispatched from the new carrier with orders to sink the Nazi if possible where she lay in Trondheim Harbour. Quite obviously this was an attempt to repeat the success of a somewhat similar action that had been mounted earlier by a force of Skuas from No 800 Squadron, Fleet Air Arm, when three hits by 500-pound bombs had sunk the cruiser *Königsberg* in Bergen Fjord for the loss of only one of the attackers, a similar price having been paid four days later for the destruction of the *Bahrenfels*, a troopship. But on this occasion, although the Royal Navy pilots pressed home their attack with great determination, only one hit was recorded by a 500-pound bomb that failed to explode, and the final hopes of the day were dashed when all but six of the aircraft were shot down by a force of Messerschmitt 109 and 110s.

Despite the relative failure of the air attack, some damage had, of course, been sustained, and it was necessary to take steps to ensure that British air-reconnaissance did not discover this. Therefore, in company with her sister ship and the *Admiral Hipper*, a plan was evolved to distract attention from the *Scharnhorst*. This took the form of the *Gneisenau* and the cruiser leaving the harbour on 20th June and entering the Iceland-Faeroes passage to divert attention from the other warship. However, it was entirely due to the hit secured by the British submarine *Clyde* (Lieutenant-Commander Ingram) 40 miles north-west of Halten that the journey had to be abandoned by the battle-cruiser.

The following day *Scharnhorst* was the centre of a fleet making for Kiel, the remaining vessels being the same destroyers that had accompanied her on 'Operation Juno' in addition to the *Greif*, *Kondor*, *Jaguar* and *Falke*, all torpedo-boats. It was on this journey that the capital ships were first subject to an attack by Fairey Swordfish aircraft of the FAA off Utsire, but in the event the strike was driven off, two of the biplanes being brought down. The ships arrived in Kiel on 23th June and there joined the *Prinz Eugen*.

Hitler's announced intention had been the use of his Navy, including its U-boat fleet and in concert with the long-range Focke-Wulf Condor aircraft, to starve Great Britain of both food and munitions, and it was therefore necessary that immediate steps be taken to prepare damaged capital ships for sea as quickly as possible. This fact was realized equally in Britain, and therefore, with two of the principal vessels in the one Baltic port, it fell to Bomber Command to raid the area.

The first of these attacks took place on the night of 1st-2nd July, and 2,000-pound bombs were used for the first time. But although hits by some smaller-calibre bombs were claimed on the *Prinz Eugen*, the larger vessel escaped unscathed. There was some confusion about what had actually taken place, no doubt due to the deliberately engineered similarity between many Nazi capital ships by this time brought about by the clipper bows and funnel caps.

This sortie was a night operation mounted by Hampdens of No 83 Squadron flying from Scampton, Lincolnshire, and while the majority bombed from 16,000 feet, one aircraft carrying a 2,000-pound SAP (semi-armour piercing) bomb was detailed to make a form of dive-bombing delivery. It is interesting to note that the pilot was Flying Officer Gibson, later Wing-Commander Guy Gibson VC, DSO and Bar, DFC and Bar.

Disregarding the balloon barrage that was known to surround the dock area, this machine made no less than six approaches to the target yet on each was unable to gain a sufficiently clear view to release the bomb. The last of these approaches ended in mishap, for hardly had the Hampden reached the end of its dive, and as Gibson hauled once more on the control column to climb for another approach, he was conscious of a different feel. The big bomb had fallen away prematurely and exploded not amongst the shipping but in the centre of Kiel town. Meanwhile the remaining machines were having to contend with an intense barrage of anti-aircraft fire.

This was of the usual type for the period, consisting of a virtual 'roof' of fire above the aircraft that was intended to force them down to a lower level where the lighter guns could deal with them with greater accuracy.

Jack Lynoch made as steady an approach as possible, waiting for the moment when the welcome words from his bomb-aimer "Bombs gone!" would announce that the bulk of the ship below had filled his sight and that the release had been pressed. It came almost at once, and the Hampden pulled up and away, sustaining a 2-foot-square hole in its tailplane from a chunk of flying shrapnel as it did so. Simultaneously the rear gunner strained his eyes into the outside darkness, all lit up by the flashes of the gun-fire, to see the results. Then, quite suddenly, the looked-for explosions came, as the stick of bombs struck home and when what was later described as "a vast shoot of reddish-yellow flame" rose from the deck.

Despite the seemingly spectacular results, the extent of the damage had to be properly assessed, and the following daylight hours found a Bristol Blenheim over the area, fitted with cameras for reconnaissance work. Even in those comparatively early days the RAF's Photographic Reconnaissance Unit was using Spitfires, polished for high speed and disarmed for this kind of work, but on this occasion the larger machine was indicated. Study of the prints at a slightly later date revealed exactly what had happened: two bombs had exploded near to the funnel, where they had undoubtedly done some damage although probably only superficially, while another had fallen in the water close by. The fourth had struck the wall of the dock, doing some damage to the masonry that could be easily repaired. This set of results illustrates only too clearly how difficult a target a relatively large vessel can be, even in the narrow confines of a dock system, a situation that is worsened when it is necessary to fly through probing searchlights and heavy anti-aircraft and pom-pom fire in order to hit it, although luckily on this occasion returning pilots were heard to remark that the "enemy night fighters were practically non-existent". But the biggest surprise was still to come, for the prints showed only a ¼-mile gap in the balloon cables through which the bombers had been flying, ignorant of the danger that lurked to each side!

Whenever possible for the remainder of 1940 these two ships, as well as the *Gneisenau*, were subject to attacks from the air, and it was not until the end of the year that Admiral Lütjens issued orders for them to break out into the North Atlantic to resume their role as commerce raiders. As events would have it, the arctic weather put a stop to these hopes after a short time at sea, when *Gneisenau* suffered storm-damage off the Norwegian coast in the severe December weather, so that a return had to be made to Kiel whence that vessel had been sent to join the others on 26th July following a torpedo-hit from a British submarine off Trondheim.

It was now imperative that the new repair-programme be carried out with maximum possible speed, and that this was done is shown by the fact that on 22nd January 1941 'Operation Berlin' was set in motion, sending the major ships hopefully towards the Atlantic. News of this was not long in reaching Britain, and three days later Admiral Tovey took the Home Fleet from Scapa in the hope of making an interception; together with eleven destroyers and eight cruisers, the fleet consisted of *Rodney* and *Nelson* with the battle-cruiser *Repulse*. The fleet lay in wait for the Nazis off the south of Iceland until 28th January, and the first sighting was made on that day, unfortunately by a depleted British flotilla since a part had been forced to leave in order to refuel. Ready for such an event, the battle-cruisers made for the Atlantic without making contact, and although a brief sighting was made by *Naiad*, the cruiser, nothing further happened. A week later *Scharnhorst* and *Gneisenau*, now commanded by Captain Fein, managed to slip through the Denmark Strait undetected.

February was scarcely a week old when the pair found themselves east of Newfoundland, and it was there that HX 106, a British convoy, was sighted escorted by *Ramillies*, the battleship—it has been since suggested that her presence influenced the Nazi admiral against making an attack. This lack of activity was made good on 22nd February when a convoy steaming west was attacked and scattered off Newfoundland, five of the ships totalling a considerable tonnage being sunk.

Early on the morning of 7th March another convoy was sighted. This was SL 67, escorted by a couple of destroyers, *Forester* and *Faulknor*, and the *Cecilia*, a corvette. The first attack was made some 3000 miles north-east of the Cape Verde Islands, but hardly had it begun than the previously unexpected presence of a battleship, HMS *Malaya*, was disclosed, and in the event action was broken off after two U-boats in the vicinity had been called to the scene.

The middle of March found the Nazi pair in the North Atlantic, and here thirteen ships were to fall victim to them, *Gneisenau*'s contribution of seven being augmented by three tankers taken captive. It was while rescuing survivors of her last sinking that *Gneisenau* was surprised by the better-armed *Rodney*, but having the advantage of superior speed, the battle-cruiser was able to decline engagement, taking the captive tankers too.

Five days later two of these, *San Casimiro* and *Bianca*, excited the attention of a Swordfish aircraft flown from the *Ark Royal*. As a result of the delayed disclosure of the discovery, no contact was made, and the battle-cruisers managed to reach Brest safely on 22nd March, escorted by the torpedo-boats *Jaguar* and *Iltis*.

This marked the beginning of the long series of attacks delivered by the RAF at the vessels lying at Brest. At a time when re-equipment and enlargement of Bomber Command was causing a virtual suspension of the air offensive, attacks directed at this target were continued, taking up as much as forty per cent of the offensive effort.

2

Leviathans Chained

When the great, grey forms of the *Scharnhorst* and *Gneisenau* finally made fast at about 7 a.m. on the evening of 22nd March 1941, it was to no haven that they had come. Brest, everyone knew, was potentially a deathtrap, but there was no alternative than to use it. There was, however, only one seeming avenue by which an attack could be made, and this was from the air, so it was reckoned that the pair could more than take care of their own defence, backed up as they were by the anti-aircraft measures of the whole dock area.

What had brought them to this state of affairs was not action on the high seas but inherent design-factors. To obtain their high speed, the diesel engines that had been the power-units of their predecessors had been abandoned in favour of steam turbines, and this high-pressure system was notoriously unreliable, so, like the *Prinz Eugen*, which was similarly powered, they lacked range, due mainly to a certain lack of bunkers, a sacrifice that had been made to ensure a large number of anti-aircraft guns. The designers were not entirely to blame for their choice of high-pressure boilers, for it must be remembered that the 'Hipper' class was the first post-war excursion into this type of vessel, unless it is argued that the pocket battleships should be classified as heavy cruisers.

The report that followed the examination of the engines of the sister ships was a gloomy one, for work on the trouble-riddled tubes in the superheaters would take almost three months to carry out. The atmosphere of gloom was deepened by the almost ceaseless rain that set in, out of which, sooner or later, everyone knew the RAF must come.

It was the night of 30th-31st March when the bombers first appeared, 109 of them, to make the first raid of a series that would go on for the next ten months, 500-pound AP bombs being dropped on this occasion. In point of fact this was not a very successful attack, and Nazi records tended to dismiss it, but even so, the hotel used as an officers' barracks in the town was hit and set alight, and neutral reports spoke of 128 casualties.

So important was the destruction of these vessels rated that a number of devices were tried out, and No 83 Squadron, now becoming very experienced in this type of work, is described as having conducted later trials with SAP bombs in conjunction with a form of illuminating the target.

This was considerably less bizarre than one tested on the huge Queen Mary Reservoir beside the Staines Road near Ashford. Those tests were a suggestion of Group-Captain Helmore's and consisted of a high-speed launch sailed without crew and controlled by radio from a Douglas P70 flying 10,000 feet above. At first the idea was no more than a series of trials conducted in general terms, but Squadron-Leader Clouston (later to rise to the rank of an Air Commodore with the DSO, DFC, AFC and Bar), who carried out most of the test-flying, quickly conceived that here was a novel method to dispose of the 'ugly sisters' by means of a small fleet of launches filled with explosives and sent into Brest Harbour by remote control. This scheme he put to Air Marshal Sir John Slessor, then in command of Coastal Command, who very properly vetoed the idea, adding, "That's fighting a private war."

Another attack on the dock complex was carried out by Bomber Command at Brest during the night of 3rd-4th April. On this occasion, as well as for the whole of the month following, mining-operations were carried out by aircraft in an attempt to seal the approaches to Brest; a total of 106 were sown during this period, not forgetting the three hundred mines that had been laid by the minelayer *Abdiel* at the end of March.

It was now plain that the method of dealing with the enemy battle-cruisers was more likely to succeed if an under-water attack was attempted, although the protective belt of 13-inch-thick (330-millimetre) armour presented a more formidable problem than the 4¼-inch (108-millimetre) decks. Consequently torpedoes rather than bombs seemed to provide the answer, so that matters immediately fell into the province of

Coastal Command. To this coming assault the bombers had made an unwitting contribution, for one of the bombs had failed to explode in the dry dock so that as a precaution the *Gneisenau* was moved into the inner harbour, Rade Abri, and moored alongside the quay there, a fact that was quickly confirmed by the visit of a Spitfire of the Photographic Reconnaissance Unit.

Precautions were also the order of the day in Britain, for knowledge of the exact progress made in the repairs to the boilers was, naturally, always scanty and often based on little more than an estimate of dock time schedules. So, in case the battle-cruisers made a sudden dash into the Atlantic, No 22 Squadron of Coastal Command, flying Bristol Beauforts from North Coates, was detailed to dispatch a small force to St Eval in Cornwall.

A sortie of this nature was exceptionally dangerous, but with the *Gneisenau* afloat it was hoped that a well-running torpedo could succeed where the night-bombing force of eleven Hampdens, four Manchesters and thirty-nine Wellingtons had failed, even after bombarding the area for 2½ hours. The early morning of 5th April had also seen the start of an abortive mission flown by ten Hampdens, which were expected to attack under cover of low cloud, but the skies had unexpectedly cleared, and they were recalled.

Early morning of 6th April found six of No 22's Beauforts prepared for take-off, but in the event only three got away, the remaining trio becoming trapped by the atrocious surface of the airfield due to their weight of weapons and fuel, although a fourth was eventually freed and set course for Brest.

The attack was planned to take the defences by surprise if possible, with a fairly low approach over the water, but the danger always existed of interception by fighters before the guns of the outer harbour had to be faced. To reduce as far as possible the chance for these to be brought to bear until the last moment, a very low approach was anticipated over the mole, and then, the torpedoes released, a steep climbing turn was to be executed in the face of the rising ground beyond, itself set about with anti-aircraft guns.

Of the four Beauforts now airborne, three failed to find the target, but one was luckier, and (with Flying Officer Kenneth Campbell, an officer of the Volunteer Reserve, at the controls,

Sergeants J. P. Scott, W. Mallis and R. W. Hillman making up the crew) the single aircraft made for the target alone. As the gunners on the three flak-ships placed at the harbour entrance as an additional defence worked like men possessed, the lone machine droned inexorably on at mast-height, only to come lower, scarcely above the deck level now, as the men at the guns wound like demons to depress their weapons. At no more than 500-yards range the torpedo dropped away, running straight and true for the side of the battle-cruiser. Almost at the same moment the Beaufort took a direct hit from one of the anti-aircraft guns and crashed into the sea, sending up a plume of spray as it did so. A moment later, the fountain of water was echoed by another, accompanied by an explosion, the sound of which was flung back by the surrounding hills.

The *Gneisenau* had taken a hit on her starboard side, damaging her plates and ribs over a distance of almost 40 feet, while the torpedo bulkhead was ripped from the thickness of the deck by the force of an explosion which at the same time damaged a propeller-shaft tunnel, contorted the gear within, smashed the bearings, wiped out the anti-aircraft control-room and damaged one of the after-turrets. As the water poured in, doing more harm, the ship began to list, and a salvage-vessel was brought alongside to pump out the water before the battle-cruiser heeled over. At the same time a search was made in the murky water of the dock for the bodies of the vanquished Beaufort crew.

Although there are exceptions, it is generally believed among fighting men that war is a ghastly enough business without politicians making it worse, and nowhere is this more true than in maritime circles, so that before long the corpses of the dead British airmen were laid on the quarterdeck of the German ship they had given their lives in the hope of destroying, and sailors stood to rigid attention with rifles at their side, mounting a respectful guard of honour over the four bundles of sodden flying-suits.

That night word was already abroad in certain circles of the last act of the gallant men, and soon it was confirmed from French spy sources, who had an experienced naval officer in their number and who monitored much of the day-to-day progress of the ships. Before long it was announced that Flying Officer Campbell had been awarded a posthumous Victoria

Cross, and Sergeant Scott a Distinguished Flying Medal.

In Germany, on the day following the attack, the faces of the Nazi Naval Staff grew long at the announcement that an inspection of the *Gneisenau*, now in dry dock, had indicated a four- to six-month repair-job.

As April advanced, it was the turn of the bombers once again to pound the leviathans, and this took the form of an attack beginning on the night of the 11th. Six well-placed bombs started fires on the mess-decks of *Gneisenau*, and there were casualties, many of them caused by splinters flung about when a further pair of bombs exploded on the side of the dock. While the dead and wounded were being taken to a number of military ambulances sent to the scene, the fire-fighting continued, but control was difficult in the confined space with little headroom between the decks, for as fast as one set seemed to be extinguished, it would quietly smoulder out of sight, only to break out again, so that one of the magazines had to be flooded as a safety-measure. The first bomb had done little more than smash in her deck plates, but the second by coincidence fell through the breach, and the third passed through the deck before exploding underneath.

Meanwhile the *Prinz Eugen* was still at sea and capable of doing execution to all enemies that crossed her course. Her next duty was to be one of the most important since it was to provide escort to the *Bismarck*, the idea being that, while she and the *Tirpitz* held the attention of British warships in the Atlantic, the *Prinz Eugen* could act as a raider in relative safety. In the event the latter's departure was delayed from Gdynia until Captain Brinkmann was satisfied that repairs to damage by a magnetic mine were satisfactorily completed. Then, on 18th May, the Fleet under Admiral Lütjens set off at the beginning of 'Operation Rheinubung', complete with an entire supply-squadron. After a brief engagement at about 8.32 p.m. with the *Norfolk* and *Suffolk* (the former coming under fire at 6½ miles range and finally disengaging under smoke), the Nazi vessels proceeded while the British Home Fleet under Admiral Tovey put to sea from Scapa Flow, 600 miles distant, with the battleship *King George V* and the carrier *Victorious*, together with the 2nd Cruiser Squadron and some destoyers, the Battle Cruiser Squadron with *Hood*, *Prince of Wales* and an escort of destroyers which had departed a little earlier.

Some 400 miles off the east coast of Greenland the opposing forces once more established contact at 5.35 a.m. on the following day. The position in which the two sides found themselves was not particularly favourable for the British vessels, for the two Nazi ships were steaming in line ahead with the *Prinz Eugen* in the lead at roughly 90 degrees to the *Hood*, with the *Prince of Wales* astern. Thus the two Germans were able to fire broadsides from eight 8-inch and eight 15-inch guns, while only the forward turrets of the British ships could be used, consisting of nine mixed 14- and 15-inch guns, since one of the latter in the fore turret of the *Prince of Wales* was out of action.

It was about 6 p.m. when the third salvo from the *Bismarck* smashed down on the thin decks of the unfortunate *Hood* and fell into the magazine. The inevitable explosion flung an inferno of flame up several hundred feet, and this was immediately replaced by a massive pall of smoke. Through the gaps in the smoke it was possible to make out the bow and stern rising in concert, indicating that *Hood*'s back was broken; evidently a high-velocity shell had found the spot where the horizontal armour round her turrets was only 2 inches thick.

The stricken vessel sank with horrifying speed, vanishing from sight in five minutes, Vice-Admiral Holland, ninety-five other officers and 1,321 men perishing; only three survivors were taken from the water. The *Prinz Eugen* was unharmed, but the *Bismarck* suffered damage to her fuel-tanks from the *Prince of Wales*'s fire, despite her shooting with the radar not functioning. The loss of oil convinced Admiral Lütjens that there could be no foray into the Atlantic now, but instead the sanctuary of Brest must be sought, and soon after this the *Prinz Eugen* was detached, unnoticed by the British seamen, to operate alone against the Atlantic convoys.

With the departure of the cruiser it would seem that the continued narrative concerning the *Bismarck* was outside the scope of this work, and such would be the case were it not that there now stepped onto the stage an actor who was to perform a major role in the drama of the Channel escape only a little later: Lieutenant-Commander Eugene Esmonde RN, an ebullient young Irishman from Drominagh in Tipperary, where he was one of six boys and a girl, himself the twin of James Esmonde.

At first it had seemed he might become a priest and perform foreign missionary work, but his teachers at the Jesuit Wimbledon College, Clongowes Wood, and St Peter's College at Freshfield agreed that his temperament of boyish good humour, hiding a thoughtful intellectualism, would be better satisfied by an active outdoor life. Therefore few were surprised when in 1928 he joined the Royal Air Force, accepting a short-service commission. It was this work that first brought him into contact with naval flying, for this was the time when maritime aircraft were still flown and maintained by RAF personnel. About five years later an opportunity occurred of his entering civil flying, and he accepted a post as a pilot with Imperial Airways, the greater part of his work taking him to India and the East.

Like so many young men of his age, Eugene was to be ultimately caught up in the meshes of the coming war and, at a time when the Admiralty had assumed control of its own air arm at last, he was offered a commission as a Lieutenant-Commander with a guarantee of fifteen years' service as a Royal Navy pilot. This he accepted, and in April 1939 he joined the training-unit at Lee-on-Solent, where he became familiar with the ubiquitous Fairey Swordfish aircraft, the type with which his squadon was equipped when it was sent to join the carrier HMS *Victorious* in the spring of 1941.

Aircraft had figured prominently in the saga of the famous battle-cruisers and the *Prinz Eugen*. Quite apart from the attentions by Bomber and Coastal Commands, it had been a routine sortie by a PRU Spitfire from Scotland that had finally rediscovered the battleship and the cruiser in the fjord not far from Bergen, and Flying Officer Suckling had seen the prints rushed to London, partly by air and finally by road, in a nightmare dash through blacked-out London. Once they had been seen by Sir Frederick Bowhill, Coastal Command's AOC, it was his orders that dispatched the mixed force of Lockheed Hudsons and Armstrong Whitworth Whitleys that pounded the vessels in their sanctuary, but without avail, due to the weather. Again, it was reconnaissance aircraft, in this case a Martin Maryland, one of the United States' less successful bombers relegated to a punishing role by the RAF, that confirmed the departure of the Nazi ships shortly after a series of intended bombing-missions had failed to discover the target in the murk.

Back at base at Hatston in the Orkney Islands, the pilot from No 771 Naval Squadron, Lieutenant N. E. Goddard RNVR, had raised the alarm, and it had become only a matter of time before the hunt was up. Thus it was fitting that aeroplanes were about to take their part in the saga.

In addition to the Swordfish, *Victorious* had aboard her Fairey Fulmars and dismantled Hawker Hurricanes, the latter for delivery to the East, but the operational and indeed only torpedo-bombers were the biplanes, and while the carrier was still about 120 miles from her quarry, nine of these, with that flown by Eugene Esmonde in the lead, took off from the heaving deck while squalls of sleet and rain added to the difficult scene. Once airborne, the crews found that their troubles were by no means over, for the aircraft, although forgiving, as might be expected with a cruising-speed of 95 knots, offered nothing in the way of comfort. The big airscrew flung back a built-in, howling gale of sodden, freezing wind, and to return fire from enemy fighters the gunner would have to stand up against the slipsteam so that the sides of his cockpit hardly reached his waist. Ahead of the machine's sole defence, the observer, in a compartment cluttered with charts, flares, boards and personal impedimenta, had to fumble with frozen fingers to obtain drift-readings, manipulate dividers, rubbers and pencils or take compass-bearing and ensure to that the pilot had not gone to sleep with the unending exertion in the numbing cold.

At about 12.30 a.m. on 24th May it was still light, for darkness falls only briefly in those latitudes. About an hour's flying rewarded Esmonde with the sight of a thin, drifting oil-slick. At first he could pick out only the *Norfolk*, *Suffolk* and *Prince of Wales*, but only a little after that the battleship loomed up. There was no doubt about the identification—another Swordfish had first spotted her twenty-five hours previously, and immediately the leading vic of biplanes separated for an attack, with Esmonde the first to go, in 5A, followed by Lieutenants Gick, in 5F, McClean, in 5B, and Pollard, in 5J. As the gun-flashes enveloped them and the vessel took evasive action, the torpedo-bombers loosed their 'fish'. Eight missed the target, but the ninth registered a hit on the point most heavily armoured, so that Nazi reports were later able to dismiss the strike as 'insignificant'. By 2.30 a.m. all the Swordfish had safely landed once more, their weary crews not knowing that within another thirty minutes the *Bismarck* was to slip away and elude pursuit. In fact the battleship had set course south-east while the searchers spread out in fan formation south-west, and bearings later taken on her wireless messages were incorrect.

Discovery was made again on 26th May by a Catalina flying-boat of No 209 Squadron flown by Flying Officer Briggs. The time was exactly 10.30 a.m. and from the course the destination of the great ship was obvious. It was little wonder therefore that the curtain of fire which greeted the Catalina did great damage, but Briggs managed to nurse the machine home to the base in Northern Ireland, carrying the news and earning himself a Distinguished Flying Cross in the process. With a couple of *Ark Royal*'s Swordfish set to shadow the target at 11.15 a.m., it was only a matter of time before an attacking-force was flown off and a formation of fourteen machines were away, after encountering the same problems as those which had beset No 825 Squadron on leaving *Victorious*.

The method of attack was one of the most devastating which can be mounted: a run-in from all points of the compass so that the senses reel—usually gunners blast away in several directions without taking proper aim. This the aircraft now did, but the pilots were surprised at the total lack of resistance. In fact there was little to be astonished about, for the reason the defenders held their fire so meekly was because the vessel that was now taking evasive action below, putting watchers in mind of nothing so much as a stricken sea-monster, was in fact the *Sheffield* and not the *Bismarck*, and it was only the violent manœuvres of the next quarter of an hour that avoided a hit.

Bismarck was still about 400 miles from Brest when the next strike came, at 8.53 p.m. on the same day, by fifteen Swordfish of No 818 Squadron after almost an hour and three-quarters' journey through a steadily descending fog. They attacked at will, every crew for itself, and of the suspected three hits reported, two were justified. The first struck a well-protected part, but despite heavy and well-directed anti-aircraft fire, the second exploded well aft, wrecking the steering-gear and jamming the rudders 15 degrees to port. *Bismarck*'s fate was sealed, and in a subsequent engagement (which marked the first use of radar for gun-control at night) the surface vessels closed in to

administer the *coup de grâce*. Firing finally ceased at 10.15 on
27th May, and at 10.36 a.m. the *Devonshire* discharged two
torpedoes at point-blank range to send the flaming shambles to
the bottom; *Bismarck* finally vanished at 11.01 a.m. at 48°10′
North, 16°12′ West. There were only 110 survivors, picked up
by *Maori* and *Dorsetshire*, although later *U-74* and *Sachsenwald*,
a weather-observation vessel, plucked a further five from the
water—seemingly the last lucky few, for a search by a Spanish
cruiser, the *Canarias*, found none.

Defeat though this action undoubtedly was, there is little that
takes place in war that does not teach a lesson of use later, and
thus it now was. The lesson was in the value of co-operation
with aircraft, and it was no more lost on Colonel Harlinghausen,
Luftwaffe Air Commander Atlantic, than it was on his enemies.
The Nazi warplanes operating from France were augmented on
this occasion by such bombing units as II/KG1, II/KG54 and
I/KG77, together with KGr100, a Heinkel 111 of which was to
damage the *Maori*.

Despite academic considerations such as these, there was no
denying the fact that the spring of 1941 was the beginning of
deeply worrying time for Hitler's navy. Just how grave the
situation was remained unclear as the final days of May ran their
course, and it was firmly believed in some circles that news
would finally filter through of the loss of the *Prinz Eugen* as well.
However, there were some more hopeful voices that suggested
she was doing no more than preserving radio silence after
slipping away from the battleship, and these proved correct as
dawn broke on 1st June, for the cruiser was suddenly sighted
approaching Brest; the story swiftly went the rounds in maritime circles that she had sustained some damage from a mine.
What was quickly known for certain was that following her
detachment from the *Bismarck* she had had to be refuelled by a
tanker waiting north-west of the area, but Captain Brinkmann
had in fact altered course and topped up the warship's tanks at
another rendezvous to the south before making for the French
peninsula. For only a short time did its docks provide some
sanctuary, for three days after the arrival of the cruiser she was
discovered by an interpreter looking through prints taken on a
routine flight by an RAF photographic reconnaissance aircraft.

With one capital ship at the bottom of the Atlantic and three bottled up in the French port, the Nazi navy was now in poor shape, but British circles realized that this ideal situation could well be short-lived. It was therefore decided to carry on the bombing-policy with, if anything, increased vigour. That decision was given increased urgency because, once all three ships were seaworthy again, they were ideally placed to carry out forays into the shipping-lanes that must be used by the Allies to take troops and much-needed supplies to the Middle East theatre, quite apart from the strong likelihood of their harassment of the lifeline of trade which stretched across the Atlantic to the United States of America.

A month to the day after entering the harbour at Brest, *Prinz Eugen* suffered the first damage from an air attack. This took place at night when a bomb that shattered the deck armour also destroyed among others the gun-control room and compass-platform, killing more than fifty of the crew and injuring about thirty. But while the subsequent inspection and report on the damage estimated six months before so much could be set to rights, the news was not all shot through with gloom for the navy of the Third Reich, as the work on the *Scharnhorst* was completed by the middle of the same month so that only sea-trials remained to be carried out. These, it was decided, were to be combined with target-practice on the 250-mile journey to La Pallice the secondary reason for the trip being to discover a new haven to replace the present one, if possible outside the range of British bombers.

When the battle-cruiser finally departed, early on the morning of 21st July, her place was taken at Brest by another ship covered by a mass of camouflage-netting to blur her outline, and the *Scharnhorst* set course south in the belief that the departure was undiscovered. This was not to be, for the unceasing reconnaissance patrols maintained by the RAF were undeceived by the false oil-slicks pointing north, and once her destination was established, a daylight attack was mounted by a force of fifteen Stirlings of Bomber Command which did some damage.

But the main attack was still to come, and it burst on Brest and La Pallice almost simultaneously at 2 p.m. on 24th May. German reports speak of a force amounting to 149 bombers, and it is certainly true that this was the heaviest attack so far carried out, for while Halifaxes dealt with the southernmost port, a

mixed force of Hampdens, Wellingtons and B17 Flying Fortresses made a hell of Brest. Although the majority were made up
of the redoubtable Barnes Wallis design, the new American
machines came in for much of the Press acclaim, despite there
being only three, and room was found in the columns of the slim
newspapers for graphic reports stating that the curvature of the
earth was visible to the young crews operating them. On balance
the raiders of La Pallice came out the more successful, scoring
five hits on the battle-cruiser that sticky afternoon and causing
severe damage to the ship's electrical system, while the inrush of
water through the bottom caused by bombs (not all of which
managed to explode) brought about a list before she was pumped
out and patched up for the return to Brest for repairs.

The bombing-force that had attacked the *Gneisenau* and
Prinz Eugen there that same afternoon achieved rather less,
perhaps because part of its load was delivered from a considerable altitude, although the buildings of the dock complex were
certainly damaged. It would be wrong to assume that these
daylight sorties were countered entirely by the enormous concentration of anti-aircraft weaponry, since fighters were also in
evidence bent on interception, but on this particular occasion
the weight of fire was out of range, below the raiders, and the
Messerschmitt fighters were reported by some of the high-flying
bombers to be seen still climbing when the attacking pilots were
setting course for base. Sixteen of the bombers failed to return;
two more were seen to crash before reaching their stations.

Twice in as many days the *Scharnhorst* had been damaged, for
'V-victor' amongst the Stirlings had claimed a hit, but almost
superhuman work by the German Navy ensured that on 26th
July she was back at the port in the Bay of Biscay, where she was
at once placed in dry dock. It was a gratifying result, and
remarks by the British aircrews (such as that concerning the
anti-aircraft fire, that "The sky over Brest looked from a distance like a huge flock of starlings") were eagerly seized on by
the British propaganda-machine, geared as it was to maintaining
public morale, and publicized with rapturous if vague descrip-
tions of the "remarkable precision" of the Sperry bombsight,
maintaining a guarded silence as to how few were employed.
Eight weeks later the much-vaunted Flying Fortresses were to
make their last operation over Europe, and part of No 90

Squadron, which had taken their trio to Brest in the summer, was detached with them to Middle East after an abortive sortie against Emden.

Such was the importance that Britain attached to the Nazi warships that during December 1941 and into the following New Year the 'Trinity' pioneer bombing-device was used in attacks. This was in fact an early and relatively crude form of the later 'Oboe'. Like the radar-assisted gunfire that had set the *Bismarck* alight, the bombing-aid was an illustration of how important 'radio location' (as it was called at about that time) was rapidly becoming; blind bombing was now possible by means of ground-controlled radar indicating a track, while a second intercepting the first gave notice of the bomb-release point acting as a target-indicator.

Stirling bombers from both 7 and 15 Squadrons flying from Oakington, Cambridgeshire and Wyton, Huntingdonshire, respectively used 'Trinity' against the fettered leviathans at the change of the year, taking with them second pilots and wireless-operators 'borrowed' from No 109 Squadron.

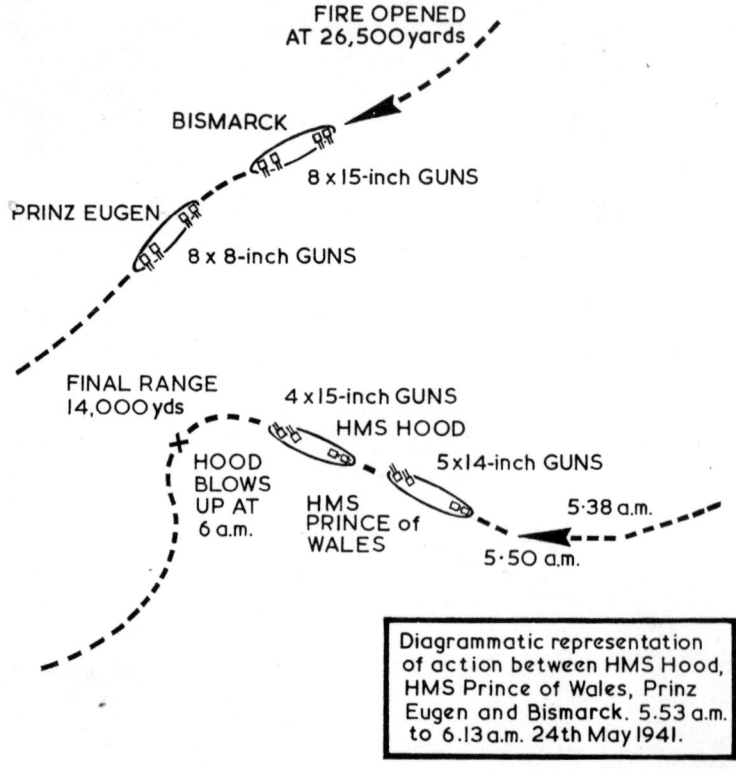

The engagement between *Prinz Eugen* and HMS *Hood*

3

Countdown

Obvious to both sides was the fact that sooner or later the condition of stalemate which existed with the three warships holed up in Brest Harbour would have to be broken, and the specific British measures, drawn up in April 1941, even anticipated those of the Nazis. Thus was born 'Operation Fuller', the plan to intercept the vessels no matter which way they set course, whether up the English Channel or even round Land's End. There was, however, one fatal flaw in all the thinking. This was the assumption, seemingly without question, that any break-out would take place during the hours of darkness, and one wonders how deeply this was affected by the assumption of senior posts by officers who, although excellent men in themselves and undoubtedly capable within the limits of their experience, were regarded at some levels as being remote from modern day-to-day issues and the men who performed them and who found it difficult to remember the days when they had been Army subalterns. Perhaps this may partially explain why, despite the early laying of plans to thwart the warships' bid for freedom, as time passed the sense of urgency faded, so that, although the watchdogs remained at their posts, their eyelids now drooped in boredom.

Involved in the counter-measures was the genial young Irish officer Eugene Esmonde, who had survived the sinking of the *Ark Royal* to which he had been transferred with his squadron and later been sent to Lee-on-Solent where No 825 Squadron was to be re-formed. In December its outlook was a somewhat doleful one, for it could muster only half-a-dozen serviceable Swordfish aircraft and only one complete crew for each, although there was one extra pilot; rather graver was the fact that of this muster only half were trained men.

This was not all. With the lesson of the destruction of the *Bismarck* still uppermost in many minds, it was assumed that the ideal way of destroying the larger ships was for them to be crippled by torpedo aircraft so that surface vessels could complete the kill, and to this end Air Marshal Joubert's Coastal Command Beauforts were kept at readiness; those of Nos 86 and 217 Squadrons were at St Eval with a detachment from the latter at Thorney Island. From Leuchars No 42 Squadron was to come south, but the transition was not to take place until early February 1942 for the move was prevented by the snow that had fallen.

Quite obviously, reports that filtered in through agents were always somewhat dated and sometimes of doubtful accuracy, so the unending photographic patrols were continued, and additionally Coastal Command maintained three patrol-lines to raise the alarm if the vessels showed signs of moving; they were code-named 'Stopper', a little to the east of the Brest peninsula, 'Line SE' and 'Habo'.

The deployment of No 825 Squadron at Manston instead of at its first base of Lee-on-Solent was brought about by a suggestion from Admiral Ramsay, the mastermind of the Dunkirk evacuation who seems to have been aware that, however formidable the British force appeared on paper, it in fact lacked the vital torpedo-bombers in any numbers. The Admiral was one of the few who believed that a daylight break would be attempted.

One factor that seemed to redress the balance was the availability of nearly 250 day bombers at various stations up and down the country, but the crews were hampered by the fact that they had received no more than casual instruction on ship-recognition, and it must be appreciated that, just as all aircraft look alike to seamen, ships are largely indistinguishable to those who fly, a fact that had already caused one near-calamity and which would do so again. Fighter Command was capable of mustering over five hundred machines, some of them capable of delivering bombs.

Meanwhile the Admiralty was laying plans for the interception by surface vessels, for the position was at first one where the only available force was made up of torpedo- and motor gun-boats at Dover, although destroyers were expected to be based at Harwich shortly, while *Manxman* and *Welshman* at Plymouth were to be held in readiness to act as fast minelayers, a duty whose importance had already been realized when another vessel of similar type, HMS *Plover*, had laid mines during the middle of January. In his capacity as Vice-Admiral, Dover, it was one of Ramsay's duties to co-ordinate this mining programme, and about a fortnight later he made a request to Coastal Command for the laying of five fields of magnetic mines along the course that it was expected the *Scharnhorst*, *Gneisenau* and *Prinz Eugen* would take off the Frisian Isles. Just how important these were to be would later become clear. The remaining fields were for the most part soon discovered, either by minesweepers or often by accident when vessels were sunk after passing through them, and those which could not be cleared were avoided by the enemy, although when the Nazi plans came to be laid in detail, the precaution was taken of sending sufficient minesweepers with the armada that accompanied the capital ships.

Within the structure of the limited resources available, all seemed set for a determined effort to oppose the passage of the Nazi vessels when and if they appeared in open waters, and any examination of the situation must be made in the light of the larger war situation at the time. As already stated, Bomber Command was in course of a vast re-equipment; abroad, Malaya was shortly to hit the newspaper headlines as a British retreat— two events that typified the larger situation of the time. Indeed, it is just possible that the deployment of the British Forces was sufficient to cope with the situation when it arose, but the weakness lay in the fact that the security screen was so close-meshed that different commands of the same service were kept in ignorance of what the others were doing. The situation was even worse when it came to co-operation between the services, which hinged largely on the degree of co-operation between individual senior officers; even this could be stymied if opposite numbers were not of like mind, and it is more than likely that at a later date the memory of this and other similar situations was lingering in the minds of the architects of the present combined Ministry of Defence.

Equally, 1941 was a period amounting almost to stalemate for Nazi Germany, which was gambling massively on the assault on the Soviet Union, so that there may have been more than slight psychological pressures for the accomplishment of something militarily grandiose at this point in time.

From his headquarters at Rastenburg in Eastern Prussia, Hitler was in personal over-all command of the war, and as 1941 drew to its close, he became obsessed with the belief that the key to victory lay in occupied Norway. Yet at much the same time he was having to cope with requests amounting almost to pressures from Admiral Raeder not only for the protection of the three vessels by the Luftwaffe while training-manœuvres were carried out in the open sea once the now-nearing date of the re-fits completion was reached, but also for the resumption of the commerce-raiding that had previously been carried on. All this had, in Hitler's mind to be reconciled not only with his personal conviction of a huge British assault on Norway but also with his faith in submarine warfare. The solution seemed simple: the Atlantic could easily be taken care of by the latter, while the ships from Brest were made use of with their big guns to repel the invaders from Norway.

It was November now, and Hitler's patience was running out—not for the first time. When Admiral Raeder paid yet another visit to his *Führer*, he was surprised to be confronted with a map.

"Here," said the Nazi leader, leaning forward over the small circular table that separated the two, "and here and here," stabbing with a forefinger at the paper, "can your ships operate in the zone of destiny."

The Admiral was astonished and realized that he must play for time if the warships were not to be relegated to little more than coastal artillery.

"Only the *Prinz Eugen* can be ready for Norway so soon, *mein Führer*," he muttered.

"Then what solution have you?" the other asked, springing to his feet.

"We could send the cruiser almost at once," answered the Admiral. "That way she would be out of danger of another repair programme after more British air raids."

He realized in a moment that he had started a train of thought, yet all he had done was to mention a half-forgotten plan in the urgency of the moment.

"Yes," replied Hitler, "yes indeed, but why only the *Eugen*?

The whole fleet could be taken out of harm's way!"

The idea seemed set in Hitler's mind when the Admiral withdrew, but in the opinion of the better-informed it was highly dangerous. Admiral Fricke, to whom Raeder communicated the proposal, was one of the most vocal in condemning it. Surely, he argued, the loss of the *Bismarck* was an object-lesson that might be repeated again—threefold, at the worst construction—if the hare-brained scheme of sending the complete group past the enemy defences was attempted.

It had been Christmas Day 1941 when the idea had last been seriously discussed, and four days later the two admirals were once again at Rastenburg. During the days between, they had not wasted their time, and at this new meeting they had decided to present reasoned evidence pointing out the potential disaster of such a course of action. For this they marshalled their arguments along three paths. Firstly, the long sojourn in Brest had meant that the greater proportion of the ships' crew were now for all intents and purposes untrained, and in order to remedy the situation a fairly protracted period of practice and training was called for. Secondly, any decision to take the three ships up the English Channel must result in the assembly of a sizeable fleet that would not only incur enormous problems of navigation but also put the entire fleet at risk from its very size. Lastly they argued that British mining had been carried out on a large scale in recent months, and once the enemy air forces and naval vessels had been alerted, there was no avenue of escape; there could be no element of surprise, for the preparations must be such as to arouse suspicion at an early date.

To these attempts at dissuasion, Hitler listened with scant patience, and when the two admirals had finished, he paused, pressing his finger-tips together as if lost in thought. When he did speak, however, the two naval officers realized that they had been wasting their time, for without hesitation the *Führer* began to harangue them on lines similar to those previously encountered, with the focal point being the imminence of a British attack on Norway that would decide the whole outcome of the war.

"The whole Fleet," he insisted, "must make their contribution to this battle, and they must be brought to the North Sea as soon as possible; the way to tackle the problem is for the Fleet to put to sea with the minimum of preparation: that way the enemy would not become unduly suspicious!"

To experienced officers such as the two present, the suggestion bordered on the suicidal, and they cast about in their minds for another course of action.

"Surely, *mein Führer*," began one, while his brain still sought a workable suggestion, "there is some alternative plan."

His leader's eyes fixed him with a steady gaze for a moment before he spoke, and in the sudden quiet the ticking of their watches seemed loud.

"Yes," replied Hitler, "yes, there is, but it would mean that the ships are paid off, their armament dismantled, and the heavy guns and their crews sent to Norway for coastal defence." He leant forward to emphasize his final words, uttered in the rising tones that had always so impressed in speeches delivered in public. "Norway is the zone of destiny. The full force of the Third Reich must be there when the British invade; it means defeat or final victory for us!"

Horrified, Raeder and Fricke withdrew, their minds spinning at the choice they had to make. On the one hand they could agree to send ships to what was almost certain disaster; on the other they had to agree to the virtual scrapping of three major vessels. That Hitler had never had much time for the Navy was well known, but this . . .

Nevertheless, Admiral Raeder was as good as his word and looked yet again into the possibilities of such a scheme, but all his efforts failed to alter his view, so that on 8th January he wrote to Hitler emphasizing his fears if the ships were sent into the North Sea in the manner suggested. As an alternative he offered to hold them at Brest until such a time as it would be of maximum advantage to send them as raiders into the Atlantic again. On the subject of taking the guns to Norway, he left no doubt as to his convictions. The concluding words of the letter were unequivocal: "Such a move . . . would help the enemy to win the war at sea."

Four days later a conference was called at '*Wolfsschanze*—the 'Wolf's Lair', in Eastern Prussia, from which the war was being personally conducted by the Nazi leader. Around the table on the fateful day was assembled an impressive galaxy of senior officers representing all the Nazi armed forces. The navy delegation was of course led by the now-weary Admiral Raeder, and it included Vice-Admiral Otto Ciliax—an unpopular Commander-in-Chief, Battleships, nicknamed 'The Black Czar' because of his stern discipline, although few realized that much of this was brought about by a painful stomach complaint. With him was his assistant, Captain Reinicke, while the dutiful Fricke and Friedrich Ruge, in charge of Western Security, completed the party.

Round the long table, the dark uniforms of the navy contrasted sharply with the lighter tones of the army and Luftwaffe, but Hitler's military jacket immediately marked him out from the others, seated at the head of the assembly. He rose and began to address his senior officers.

Perhaps the majority were interested—they certainly kept masks of polite thought across their faces, but for the two admirals it was the same story of the immediate danger to occupied Norway, to the defence of which all resources must be diverted. He concluded with an outline of the idea to send the *Scharnhorst*, *Gneisenau* and *Prinz Eugen* out of Brest and up the English Channel with such despatch that the enemy would be taken by surprise and in consequence fail to react in time.

When his leader had finished, it was the turn of Otto Ciliax to speak, and he rose heavily and paused for a moment, eyeing the assembly, his gaze resting a moment longer than necessary on Hans Jeschonnek, Luftwaffe Chief of General Staff, who must guarantee air-cover if Hitler's plan was accepted. Then the Vice-Admiral spoke, and his opening words finally dashed any lingering hopes the others might have cherished that the ships were not to be sent to their seeming doom.

Such a plan, he stated, had in daylight a far greater chance of succeeding than one to send the fleet on the far longer and therefore more dangerous trip right round the British Isles. However, such a course of action, he added with a glance at the Luftwaffe officer, would depend on an effective fighter cover and a swept channel through the known minefields.

He sat down and looked at the others, waiting for their support. It was Commodore Ruge who first gave it.

The menace from mines was a very real one, he said, but the danger they present had been exaggerated. The real problem lay in the observation of large numbers of minesweepers alerting the enemy, but he thought that this could be overcome if they conducted their operations in small concentrated groups. Any channels that his vessels cleared would not, he added, be in any measure one hundred per cent safe, but the danger would be greatly reduced if sweeps beforehand were carried out in the manner suggested.

Lieutenant-General Jeschonnek then spoke. He agreed that something in the region of 250 daylight fighters could be provided, but he had misgivings if there would be sufficient numbers available both to provide cover and to take on enemy aircraft in the battles that were certain to develop. In this he was supported by Colonel Galland, no chairborne officer but a practical fighting man, who spoke from experience when he pointed out the problems that were posed when the Luftwaffe's long-range fighters were met by the strong formations that Britain had at her disposal.

But the breathtaking suggestion of a daylight bid for freedom had impressed in varying measure all of those present, and the non-maritime officers agreed on the boldness of a plan to take the ships out of Brest under cover of darkness at such an hour that they would have to pass up the narrowest part of the English Channel in whatever grey light the winter day would provide. It was left to Otto Ciliax to bring the assembly back to reality again by an application of his seaman's logic. He leaned across the table and exchanged a few words with the able Grand Admiral Raeder, and it was the latter who spoke next.

"The tide and available daylight will decide the time of departure," he remarked dryly, and a silence descended on the seated group.

It was Hitler who broke the hush, speaking briskly, almost happily; now that his decision had been vindicated by an experienced seaman, he was anxious to take advantage of the situation.

"The very boldness of the plan augurs well for its success," he declared, adding, "The British are incapable of making swift decisions, still less of carrying them out."

He then went on to justify the step that was about to be taken, pointing out that to leave the vessels in Brest Harbour would only be to invite further air attacks; perhaps one would not survive the Channel run, possibly more, but if they remained

where they were, it was only a matter of time before they were
finally put out of action; this way there was hope of some
measure of success. He then repeated the theory that the de-
cisive battles of the war were about to take place in Norway, and
everything must be diverted to ensure victory there.

Having emphasized this point yet again, Hitler then returned
to the details of the release of the three ships. The element of
surprise was vital, he assured them, and the move must be made
as soon as possible. He added, "Even if one or more is not
seaworthy, the others must go." The only provision, he said,
was that, if only the *Prinz Eugen* was ready for the journey, she
must not go alone.

Thus the final decision was made, and the Operation which
was to be code-named 'Cerberus' was born. With the great
decision taken, there was evident an atmosphere almost of relief
among the gathering which was entertained to dinner by Hitler
afterwards in the air-conditioned gloom of the concrete strong-
hold underneath '*Wolfsschanze*'.

As has already been stated, the preparations were to be kept
to a minimum, and these were concerned mainly with minesweeping, but there were other measures to be taken as well.
One of the largest was the despatch of a large number of
marker-vessels, sixteen in all, and mainly minelayers sent off to
indicate the safe passage along which the fleet was to pass
between Le Touquet and Heligoland. There were other steps
that were intended but not carried out due to the weather, for by
and large it was cold, with some snow and poor visibility during
the days that preceded the planned departure, so that the
concentrated series of attacks on the bases of the British torpedo-bombers that had been demanded by Otto Ciliax were not
carried out.

As the days passed, the work on all three ships was stepped
up, so that it was carried on without cessation, day and night,
using trusted labour and not that provided by French dock-
workers who had been known to work as slowly as possible to
frustrate the Nazi plans. It was not long before it became
evident that not one or two but all the capital ships would be
ready to make their departure from Brest before the middle of
February. There were those who pointed out that the code-
name had been well chosen, for was Cerberus not the three-

headed monster of Greek mythology? The fact that he acted as a sentinel for the underworld was probably best ignored, at least in Nazi Germany—although it probably crossed the minds of more than one Briton or Frenchman who was sufficiently close to the world of espionage to hear such matters!

Just how valuable a contribution was made to the widening British picture of the situation from this source will, without question at this point in time, never be fully known, even had it ever been possible, but it certainly existed and may have been one of the reasons, apart from the indications of moon, tides and season, why a report issued in January 1942 spoke of the battle-cruisers and the 'Hipper'-class vessel being ready for sea after the 24th of that month. But there were other signs that contributed, among them the noted increase of minesweeping, despite all the precautions that were taking place to mask the fact, particularly in the region of Brest; this, allied to reports of unusual activity by E-boats (known in Germany as S-boats), together with destroyers, greatly increased British suspicions.

At this juncture there was no reason to believe that a forced passage up the Channel would be chosen in favour of the longer route ending in the Atlantic, but it was agreed in British naval circles that the former was the more attractive. Not only was it shorter but the distance involved on the alternative course would effectively cancel out any possibility of air cover by the more manœuvrable short-range aircraft.

Sir Philip Joubert, the C-in-C, Coastal Command, had, at the beginning of February, given notice of the worsening situation when he drew attention to the growing number of destroyers and torpedo boats in the vicinity of the French harbour, and he concluded with the warning that the likely conditions prevailing about 10th-15th February were all in favour of the enemy vessels making the hazardous passage up the Channel. He pointed out that, since the three capital ships had been observed taking part in exercises in the open water in the immediately preceding period, it would be reasonable to assume that a break-out attempt would not be long in coming. 15th February was suggested as a tentative date when there would be no moon. In this, Sir Philip was in complete accord with the opinions shared between Bomber, Fighter and Coastal Commands of the Royal Air Force, the Air Ministry and the Admiralty. An assumption that had remained unchallenged for so long that it was now taken as established fact was that the bid would be made under cover of darkness, a time when the meagre torpedo-bomber units stood a greater chance of success. It seems that there were only two naval officers, one in Britain and the other in Germany, who were sufficiently bold to think differently.

The second of these was, of course, Admiral Ciliax and the greater part of the preparations in the maritime sphere fell to his lot. First and foremost among his responsibilities was the renewed training of the ships' crews, for to the men the vessels had by this time become little more than work to which they were taken daily for their duties, the whole of their off-duty time being spent in barracks ashore for reasons of safety. In addition to this the original crews had been severely reduced, and experienced men sent elsewhere had been replaced by others who had taken part in little training on board; the total sea-time of many amounted to only the few days when the *Scharnhorst*, *Gneisenau* and *Prinz Eugen* had taken part in sea-trials. Apart from practical measures such as this, there were also tactical preparations to be made, and these must of necessity concentrate on the avoidance—or reduction, as far as possible of anticipated enemy resistance. It was common knowledge in Nazi circles that Dover was the base of a torpedo-boat squadron, and since these constituted a very real danger to the survival of the German ships, it therefore followed that an attempt must be made to reduce the striking-power from this direction. The only manner in which this could be done was to decoy Vice-Admiral Ramsay's boats into the open water and to destroy as many as possible in an open fight; so that no replacements could be made before the departure of the Nazi fleet, such an operation must be undertaken as near the chosen date as possible. Consequently on 11th February a flotilla of E-boats was sent to act as bait in the waters off the coast of Dungeness. Throughout the grim overture that was being played as a curtain-raiser to the larger encounter to come, one is impressed by the almost equal experience behind the so-called 'Black Czar' and the Vice-Admiral, Dover, for the latter refused to be drawn and committed only his MGBs to the encounter, and the subsequent engagement was fought inconclusively by the light of flares dropped by coastal aircraft so that the E-boats finally withdrew in the morning after a negative result.

On the larger canvas of which operations such as this were no more than a detail, there was still much work to be done, and despite the extent and breadth of the undertaking it was vital that all should be carried out under the greatest possible secrecy. With a sudden flash of humour, Hitler had suggested that the swiftest way of drawing a red herring across the path of British Intelligence was to inform Mussolini 'in confidence' that the three vessels were about to be despatched to the Pacific to assist the Japanese! More practical was the measure whereby the Operation was, at different times, described under five code-names, of which 'Cerberus' was only the final one.

All this work had to be done under the unending threat of air attack, and Nazi sources were claiming the destruction of forty-three aircraft on these sorties alone, accounting for 247 crew-members.

With the prevailing tide running eastwards, it was regarded as possible for the fleet to make an average speed of 27 knots, and this in turn was dependent on the actual channel selected. Since it is possible for a vessel to reach its higher speeds only in relatively deep water, the marker-boats were finally dispatched to indicate a course that would give a depth of not less than 15 fathoms, and from this no less than 119 mines of all types were finally cleared, eighty vessels being diverted to this operation alone.

Hitler's demand that a minimum of 250 aircraft form an umbrella over the fleet at all times posed something of a problem for General Jeschonnek, one of the senior officers who had been present at the fateful conference at 'Wolf's Lair', but the method of overcoming this was to use thirty ME110 night fighters at the beginning and towards the end of the operation when the light would be seasonably poor. The control and, indeed, the direction of such a large number of aircraft in a relatively small air space had to be very carefully formulated. The Luftwaffe side of the sortie was given the separate code-name of 'Thunderbolt'.

To maintain a continuous cover of fighters, it was decided to divide the escort into two groups operating with sixteen machines at high and low levels. The length of time that these could spend over the ships naturally depended on the amount of fighting involved, since sufficient fuel had to be husbanded for the return to base, and this would vary according to the position of the fleet, a factor which would also make a difference to the arrival-time of replacements. With luck these patrols could spend a little over half an hour over the fleet, and so, to give as great a margin as possible to the hand-over time, new formations were scheduled to arrive ten minutes before the departure time of the 'old guard', so that if fuel was not running short for the latter, there could be at any one time a maximum of thirty-two machines in the air space above the vessels.

The strain that such a schedule placed on the ground crews was enormous; not only had the maximum number of fighters to be airworthy at the beginning of the operation but the turn-round time for returning fighters to be prepared for the next sortie was never greater than thirty minutes. In this manner it was ensured that there would always be enough fighters to reinforce the standing patrols to intercept the direct attacks from British aircraft that must come.

The fighters were drawn entirely from units equipped with Messerschmitt 109s and Focke-Wulf 190s, and these were in the main found by JG 2 and JG 26 based on the Channel coast with ninety machines each; to Le Havre went a temporary detachment of a dozen Messerschmitt 109s from the fighter school at Paris. To this fighter force was added the strength of JG 1 based in north-west Germany, although these could not be utilized until comparatively late in the day due to range considerations and from the fact that, on the morning following the main part of the operation, the sixty fighters of this unit were to provide escort for the final part of the journey. The total was just two aircraft in excess of the requisite number of 250.

However, these aircraft constituted only the fighter force, and it was anticipated that British attempts to stop the convoy would involve surface vessels as well; therefore 176 bombers from Luftflotte 3 were detailed to cope with this aspect of the coming encounter. Until only a few hours beforehand none of those working like beavers to prepare the machines had any idea what plans were being laid, so close was the security-net drawn about the operation, and the rumour-carriers in the German service messes had to be content with the exchanged assurances that it was 'something big'.

Both British and German authorities were in effect agreed on the probable date for the break-out, but the final selection of an exact hour must depend on the all-important weather. Chiefly because it provided a time comfortably within the period of maximum darkness, 12th February seemed to be the ideal choice. The reason for this date was also because it offered convenient high water at Dover; with the highest tide arriving at 9.30 a.m., the choice seemed ideal—ideal, this is, if only the weather for that date offered the same advantages. The reports transmitted from the three U-boats in the Eastern Atlantic were studied with more than normal interest. With a westerly wind that would bring the depression forming south of Ireland into the Channel by the early hours of the morning, this would have the effect after a few hours of presenting poor weather over aerodromes and bases in the British Isles while in the Channel it would pass after a few hours. The sea was predicted to be slight to moderate with the wind not exceeding 13 mph. But visibility was forecast to be no more than a maximum of 10 miles, and at altitude the cloud was predicted to be ten-tenths. In the event, the majority of these forecasts were correct, although several hours late, and perhaps in the spirit that prompted the Luftwaffe to nickname the meteorological service 'false prophets', the final decision was taken that 12th February was the day; the reports from the long-range Focke-Wulf 200 aircraft seemed to confirm what the weather-submarines had said: 'Operation Cerberus' and its attendant 'Thunderbolt' were 'on'.

The last operational conferences were held, and armed guards attracted the attention of sullen Parisians as they paced before the doors of the Palais Luxembourg where the last decisions were being taken. From this senior officers dispersed to brief their commanders in northern France, where the snow still lay on the freezing ground, and to issue sealed orders after revealing the nature of the mission that the next day would bring.

All was secret bustle as the ships due to make up the screens made towards their rendezvous. A flotilla of E-boats closed in on Cherbourg to form part of the escort, and at 6.30 p.m. six destroyers of the 5th Flotilla slipped into position with decks cleared for action. On board the first, *Z-29*, was Rear-Admiral Bey, the Officer Commanding, and this was followed by the

Richard Beitzen carrying the Flotilla Commander, Captain Berger. Following these came the *Paul Jacobi*, the *Hermann Schömann*, the *Friedrich Ihn* and *Z-25*. On board the *Scharnhorst* (Captain Hoffmann), the *Gneisenau* (Captain Fein) and the *Prinz Eugen* (Captain Brinkmann) all was expectancy, and the atmosphere was heightened on the flagship by its use as floating command-post for the protective fighters, with *Oberst* Ihel assisted by experienced fighter pilots, and *Oberst* Elle in command of the radio crew.

Then, with the darkness deepened by the blackout adding a touch of drama, hundreds of pairs of eyes watched the hour approach. Exactly at 7 a.m. cables were slipped, and the three ships stole from their berths towards the destroyers waiting at the harbour entrance. Hardly had they made much progress than a warbling note sounded across the docks: an air-raid warning! The three moved back to their moorings again and tied up while from some 7,000 feet the first bombs began to fall from the twenty or so RAF raiders as the searchlights probed into the blackness and the anti-aircraft guns on the ships and ashore filled the sky with shrapnel.

4

Inglorious Twelth

Linchpin of the British hopes of intercepting the three Nazi warships was the system of aircraft patrol-lines which, long planned, began to be flown each night from 3rd February. Of these three the most important was that farthest to the west, from Brest itself to the island of Ushant, and hopefully called 'Stopper'. From this point a second, 'Line SE', ran to the Ile de Bréhat off the north-easterly point of Brittany, while the third part of the system ran from the east side of the Cherbourg peninsula at Le Havre to Boulogne and was known as 'Habo'. All were flown by Lockheed Hudson aircraft fitted with radar reputedly capable of spotting a vessel of any size at 30 miles' distance.

Whatever the truth of this, it failed to take into consideration the human element, for the aircrews expected to operate this patrol system had not received sufficient training; to this must be added the fact that a glance at the map will show that there was no overlap, which would to some extent have made compensation for the lack of crew experience, so that the full responsibility rested with the men in a single machine, a fact that points to a blind belief in the range claimed for the radar system.

The air raid that had caused the three ships to tie up at their old berths again lasted only an hour and a half. Almost immediately after the welcome notes of the 'Raiders Past' siren had died away, an order went out for details of harm to the capital vessels. It seemed almost a miracle that all reported no damage, so that without more ado Admiral Ciliax was signalling all captains to prepare to put to sea within the hour. The time was now exactly 9 a.m. and a few minutes before 10 a.m. the trio was passing out of the harbour to begin the journey. What no one knew at the time, least of all the officers and men of the ships now embarked on the first leg of the journey, was that the insistent pressure that Hitler had brought to bear on his advisers to carry out this mission was genuinely activated by a concern for the course of the war in Scandinavia—not that anyone believed it to be the 'zone of destiny' it was claimed to be but because in Norway work was being conducted in connection with 'heavy water', the vital factor necessary for atomic fission, and later the production of a Nazi atomic bomb.

Just before the sirens had sounded over Brest, one of the Hudson patrol aircraft was taking off from the Coastal Command station of St Eval in Cornwall. It was a machine of No 224 Squadron.

The first encounter with the enemy that night was when, in the extreme blackness brought about by the complete lack of a moon, the British plane nearly collided with a Junkers 88. As the pilot took evasive action, the radar was turned off, and when normal patrolling was resumed, the set refused to function, despite the prolonged efforts of the three sergeants who made up the crew. With a dead radar set there was no point in continuing—the night was far too dark for visual observation, and so the plane returned to St Eval; a landing was made after 7.30 p.m.

According to all the claims made for the radar, the ships should have shown up as distinct 'blips' in the scan of the replacement Hudson which was over the Brest area a few minutes before the ships left, but the screens showed nothing. At this point in time it is only too easy for armchair tacticians to argue the point, but it must be faced that the exact time, to the minute, of the Nazi departure is the subject of several differing reports, and those few minutes are vital.

Meanwhile the gremlins were having a field-day in another Hudson machine, that sent to patrol the 'Line SE'. It had arrived on its patrol line at a little after 7.30 p.m. on 11th February, and the radar was switched on. At 8.55 p.m. the pilot was informed that the set had failed and that efforts to discover the fault had achieved nothing. Despite this it was decided to patrol the Bréhat to Ushant line in the hope of something being spotted visually, but the night was so dark that this was impossible. At 9.56 p.m., an hour after the report of the electronics failure, it was therefore decided to return to base.

It was at this point that the first major error was made, for after the Hudson had landed and the technicians had begun their search, no attempt was made to replace the watcher in the sky, and 'Line SE' went unattended on the very night that the ships which were the reason for its existence were about to move. Worse, Admiral Ramsay was kept in ignorance of the situation as no report was sent on the matter.

As we have already seen, there existed a third patrol line, 'Habo', policed by, once more, Lockheed Hudson aircraft, this time of No 223 Squadron operating out of Thorney Island. Two machines maintained the watch that night, but at no time during the hours of duty (which ceased early for the second machine, just after 6.30 a.m. on the morning of 12th February) was the enemy formation ever within range of its radar.

However, it would be wrong to assume that the responsibility for keeping an eye on the Nazi fleet rested entirely on Coastal Command or even the RAF as a whole, for the Royal Navy was also making its contribution—or at least as much of a contribution as the war situation allowed, a state of affairs that affected the whole provision of 'Operation Fuller' as the hoped-for interception was coded.

This extra line of watch was maintained by three submarines. Two of them were elderly H-boats, and their beat was confined to the Bay of Biscay, but the third was a modern type, HMS *Sealion*, her captain, Lieutenant-Commander Colvin, under orders to watch the immediate area of Brest.

At first it may seem that the allocation of only one submarine of modern design to such an important duty indicated a certain negligence in the light of the importance of the quarry, but this was by no means the case; the Navy was perfectly aware of the gravity of the situation that would exist if the 'Fuller' measures allowed any one of the three Nazi capital ships to get back into the Atlantic, then or at a later date. (The total of nearly twelve thousand service men transported, homeward or outward, in only three convoys during just the preceding month was ample proof of this.) The reason for the seeming low priority given to the patrols was that the more modern vessels had perforce to be sent as replacements for the heavy losses incurred in the Mediterranean, leaving just the two old vessels normally used for training and *Sealion*. The latter was operating directly under orders from Vice-Admiral Sir Max Horton, the Flag Officer, Submarines, and it was hoped that at some point Colvin would be able to penetrate Brest Roads and torpedo one of the Nazi ships while engaged on open-water trials there.

Brittany's coast here is strongly reminiscent of that of Cornwall, and although there were certain advantages to be gained from this, it was also true that both Normandy and Brittany had tides that made station-keeping a difficult matter. Notwithstanding, 7th February found *Sealion* within the natural sweep of the bay in daylight, and, observations indicating no activity, her commander decided to wait until the fall of darkness in case something happened. Except for a near-discovery by a hunting Dornier 215, nothing of interest happened, and an air of relaxation began to be noticed among the largely inexperienced crew.

Perhaps the Dornier had seen, or at least suspected, more than they realized, for before long all were alerted by the announcement that approaching propellers could be heard.

In the pregnant silence that followed, every man could hear his own heart beating, and the tension of their eardrums seemed to blot out silence with an atmospheric-like hiss. Then just a suggestion of another sound took over, and a slight hollow-sounding vibration was audible. It came nearer; plain now, it was the reverberating boom with metallic overtones of depth-charges. There was no time to be lost; a sunken submarine with a dead crew, however gallant, is of no use to any commander, and so, with as little disturbance as possible, the vessels quietly slipped into the open sea as the dread sound faded away in the hostile waters outside the hull.

Despite the nightly necessity of a retreat to recharge batteries, it was planned to take advantage of the tide to repeat this performance on subsequent nights, and the last of these was to take place at dusk on the fateful 11th February. All went according to plan, and at a little past 7 p.m. *Sealion* moved silently into place; the inevitable waiting began. At just the moment when the original break-out time was seeing the docks suddenly become a hive of industry, as the three ships slipped their moorings, there, in the narrow passage through which they must pass, a British submarine lay in wait with torpedo-tubes charged.

Then from the direction of the dock complex came the sound of a siren and soon after the noises of a bombing-raid, the same one that was to cause the enemy fleet to return to harbour while the twenty-five machines did their worst. The RAF had unwittingly saved the *Scharnhorst, Gneisenau* and *Prinz Eugen* from the hands of the Royal Navy. Before it was safe for the vessels to resume their delayed journey, the pressing needs of the batter ies had forced *Sealion* to seek the open sea once more.

Despite the late start, the three ships with their escort of destroyers was making good time. It looked as if they would be back on schedule before long and at 1.14 a.m. on 12th February for the first long leg of the run up the Channel in the direction of Alderney, about four hours distant. The escort too was growing, and, with first light roughly in the vicinity of the Cherbourg peninsula, they would be joined by the 2nd Torpedo Boat Flotilla under Commander Erdmann, from Le Havre, comprising *T2, T4, T5, T11* and *T12*. From Dunkirk, Commander Wilcke was later to bring the 3rd Flotilla, formed by four more torpedo-boats, *T13, T15, T16* and *T17*, all to become components of the outer screen.

At the narrowest point of the English Channel more vessels were to join the Fleet—Commander Schmidt's 5th Torpedo Boat Flotilla made up of *Falke, Iltis, Jaguar, Kondor* and *Seeadler* at Cape Gris Nez. Before this point was reached, there would be other additions in the form of escort-craft, mainly E-boats and R-boats, the large multi-purpose coastal motor-launches with a maximum speed of 21 knots of which forty had been built up to that time at various dates since the first was taken on charge in 1934. Further west, the protection given by surface-vessels was to come from both the Naval Defence Force for the area and Naval Forces North with the Torpedo Boat Flotillas of Lieutenant-Commanders Feldt, Bätge and Obermaier, under orders to augment the protective screens.

All these vessels would, in the main, be providing protection over and above that which the three capital ships were capable of mustering themselves against hostile shipping, but the danger of attack from the air was a very real one. Although responsibility for air cover fell naturally enough to the Luftwaffe, as already described, this was not regarded as the only means of beating off attackers, and therefore among the preparations carried out on all three of the large vessels had been an increase of the number of anti-aircraft guns, some of them even being mounted on the mast platforms to deal the more effectively with low-flying torpedo-bombers. The degree of importance attached to this defence can best be shown by reference to the total of fifty-six 20-millimetre-calibre guns installed for the *Prinz Eugen*'s Channel venture and the addition of an extra sixteen weapons of similar type in batteries of four on the *Scharnhorst* and *Gneisenau*, one group being retained when the special armament was later dismantled.

Aboard his leading flagship, Admiral Ciliax might well be excused if he believed that the smoothness with which the operation had gone up to now was the result of the meticulous planning of the last few weeks. Even the relatively good visibility ahead seemed as much a part of the plan as the spring tide taking them steadily eastward with the prevailing current.

As the ships, with their greater concentration of protective vessels to their port (and therefore British) side made good headway past the Cape de la Hague at about 7.14 a.m., the first fighters were taking off into the darkness—twin-motor Messerschmitt 110 with crews trained in the art of fighting between dusk and dawn. Thirty-six minutes later, under a cloud-base at 1,500 feet they were in position, comforting 'angels' flying so low that it seemed to the now-doubled look-outs that it was almost possible to touch them.

Dawn was breaking, and with it began the time of maximum danger, but for the moment the men in the exposed positions on deck and superstructure had little to do save stamp their feet in the cold; if murmured conversations were carried on, the subject might be the speech appealing to their patriotism and fighting spirit from the Admiral which had been relayed over the internal-communications system at midnight, a final unreal touch to a hellish evening made the more unbelievable by the return to Brest docks where the smoke canisters had flung a choking grey-green blanket over all in an effort to protect them.

Meanwhile, all was not going quite so well as it at first seemed, for British radar was becoming increasingly alive to the fact that something was afoot in the Channel. The Nazis were only too aware that these electronic watchdogs could be their undoing, and special measures were to be taken to meet the threat, but for some reason jamming from land transmitters was not ordered to begin until 9 a.m., probably as another attempt not to raise too much suspicion. Be that as it may, there was left a time-gap when the tell-tale 'blips' on British screens could well spell disaster.

The reason for this was that there existed a gap in the jamming-system unknown to the enemy, the explanation being that he was aware only of the existence of M-sets, the older-style system identified by its massive H-style aerials, and stations thus equipped were already reporting interference. This would have been due to the attentions of a couple of Heinkel 111s that had taken off from their base near Paris, fitted with jammers designed to give the same signal as a group of aircraft circling. But the newer—type 271K—sets working on short-wave were undeceived by the pair of bombers patrolling over the Channel, and it was one of these which registered a movement too fast for shipping and therefore obviously aircraft. Yet, while one by one the radar-stations changed frequency or finally switched off, some of them to use the newer sets, nothing was done at the time to investigate the matter further, mainly because after a short while the signal seemed to fade. In fact, what they had picked up was the reflection from the night fighters over the shipping which, although certainly flying low, were not taking the risks that would have been present if they had obeyed orders too exactly in the poor light which were to patrol at zero feet, thus being below the limit of the scan. None of this, however, excited any particular comment. Although individual officers in the operations rooms had their suspicions, ignorance of the whole matter among those to whom they spoke, a case of security gone mad, or 'stone-walling' by juniors blocking access to the higher echelons, frustrated attempts to sort the matter out. Although it is only too simple at such a distance in time to be sage after the event, equally guilty were the officers whose suspicions were aroused, surely one of the few cases when an attempt to 'pull their rank' would have been justified.

Meantime the fleet was making good progress and had largely made up the time lost due to the late start, so that it was roughly off Dieppe. Here the gods who seemed to be protecting the project up to now decided to inject a note of tension, for it was discovered that ahead lay an undiscovered minefield. Four sweepers under Lieutenant-Commander Bergelt were hurriedly summoned, and almost superhuman efforts managed to clear a narrow passage. With a speed reduction to something like 10 knots, the vessels made their cautious way through without incident.

By this time day fighters had taken up position in the protective umbrella, and at different stations about thirty extra machines were held in reserve. Some of these remained grounded for the whole day by snow flurries driven by strong gales across the fields, although the pilots remained strapped in and with engines warm ready to be airborne at one minute's notice.

The fleet was now just about back on schedule, and this fact alone removed some of the strain on the waiting pilots, for it was at one time believed that the late start would mean the transfer of the bulk of the fighters from the Calais sector westward to Caen, Cherbourg and Le Havre.

High up on the windy cliffs overlooking Dover, bleak at that time of year, stood (and still remains) the radar station that overlooks the Swingate Downs from where the first four Royal Flying Corps Squadrons had staggered off to France twenty-eight years before. This station was one of those equipped since about three months before with the short-wave Type 271 radar set, and after the enemy fleet had been at sea for more than ten hours, three tell-tale blips on the screen indicated the presence of something 'pretty big' in the Channel about 60 miles distant. The station-commander, Flight-Lieutenant Kidd, immediately decided that something must be done—and at once, so he tried to telephone Dover Castle on his direct line. When this proved dead, he resorted to the scrambler, which was equally inoperative, so, fuming with frustration at the waste of time and with muttered comments about the efficiency of Post Office telephone engineers in general, he made a round-about call via Portsmouth.

Almost simultaneously at Biggin Hill, where no one anticipated flying due to the weather, a fresh controller was coming on duty. At the best of times, work in an operations room is wearisome, and the slow progress of plaques and counters across the map can be soporific, but the glance that the Squadron-Leader gave to the main table came from fresh eyes, and he

Gneisenau after the refit with funnel cowl and clipper bows. A dark grey camouflage was applied to the main part of the hull with a lighter tone to the bows and stern, thus foreshortening the apparent length.

Prinz Eugen seen after surrender at Copenhagen on 25th May 1945. This view emphasizes the reason why she was often mistaken by British observers for one of the battle-cruisers.

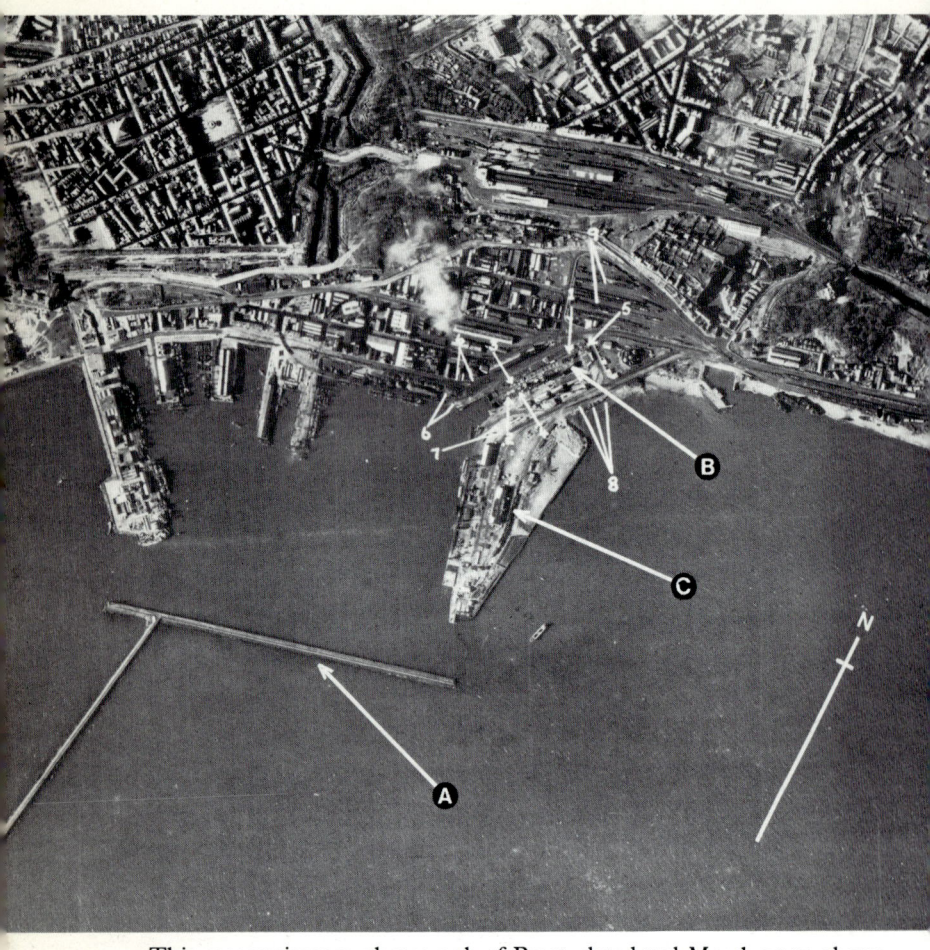

This reconnaissance photograph of Brest, dated 3rd March 1941, shows 'A', an uncluttered mole, 'B', a 'Hipper'-class cruiser, undoubtedly the *Prinz Eugen*, and 'C', a warehouse with a holed roof brought about by bombing, The white numerals are wartime photo-interpreters' marks.

Opposite: The same area three months later. The mole has now gained what is probably a row of smoke-screen canisters at 'A', and the cruiser is still in place, but 'C', the warehouse, has had its roof repaired.

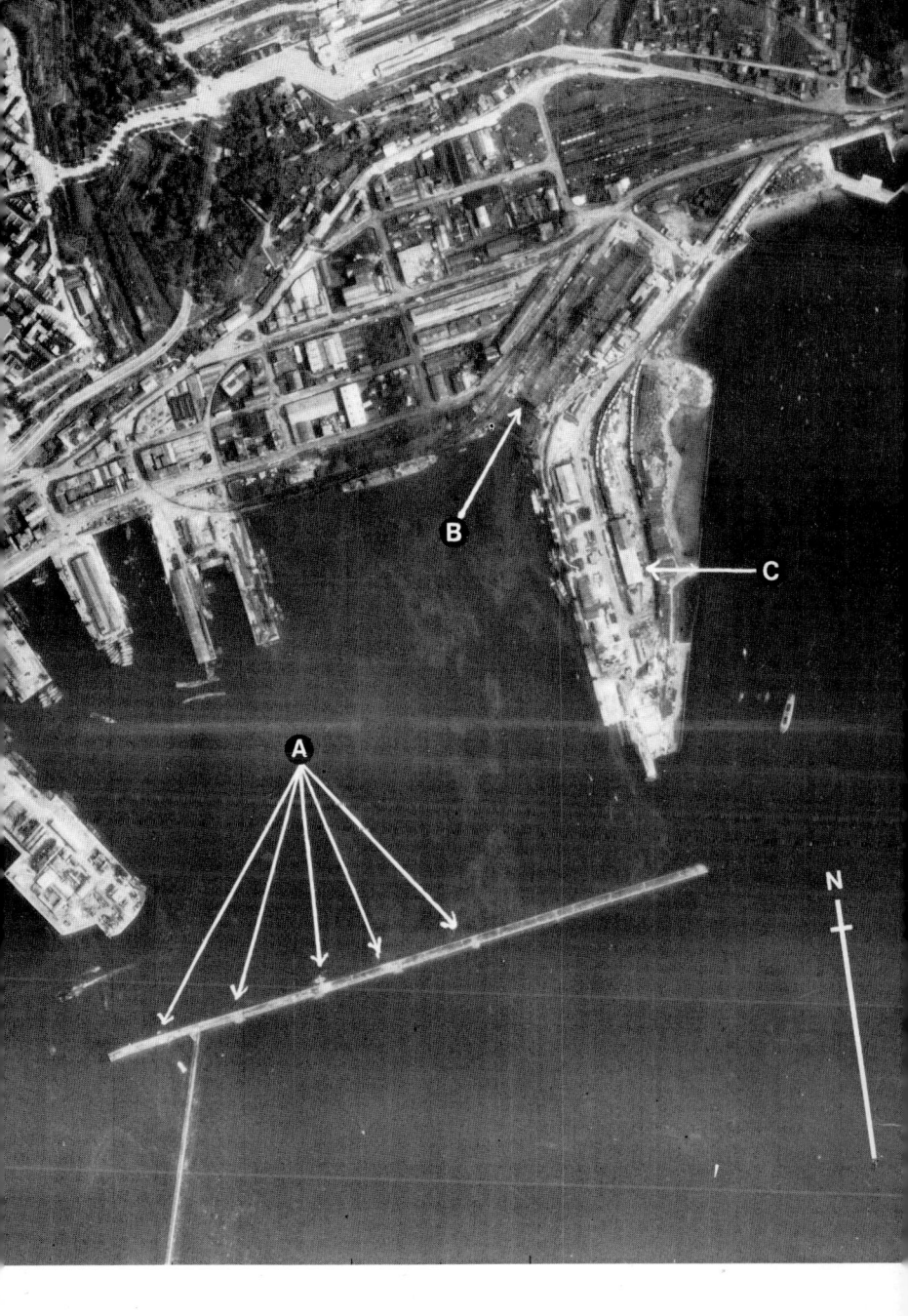

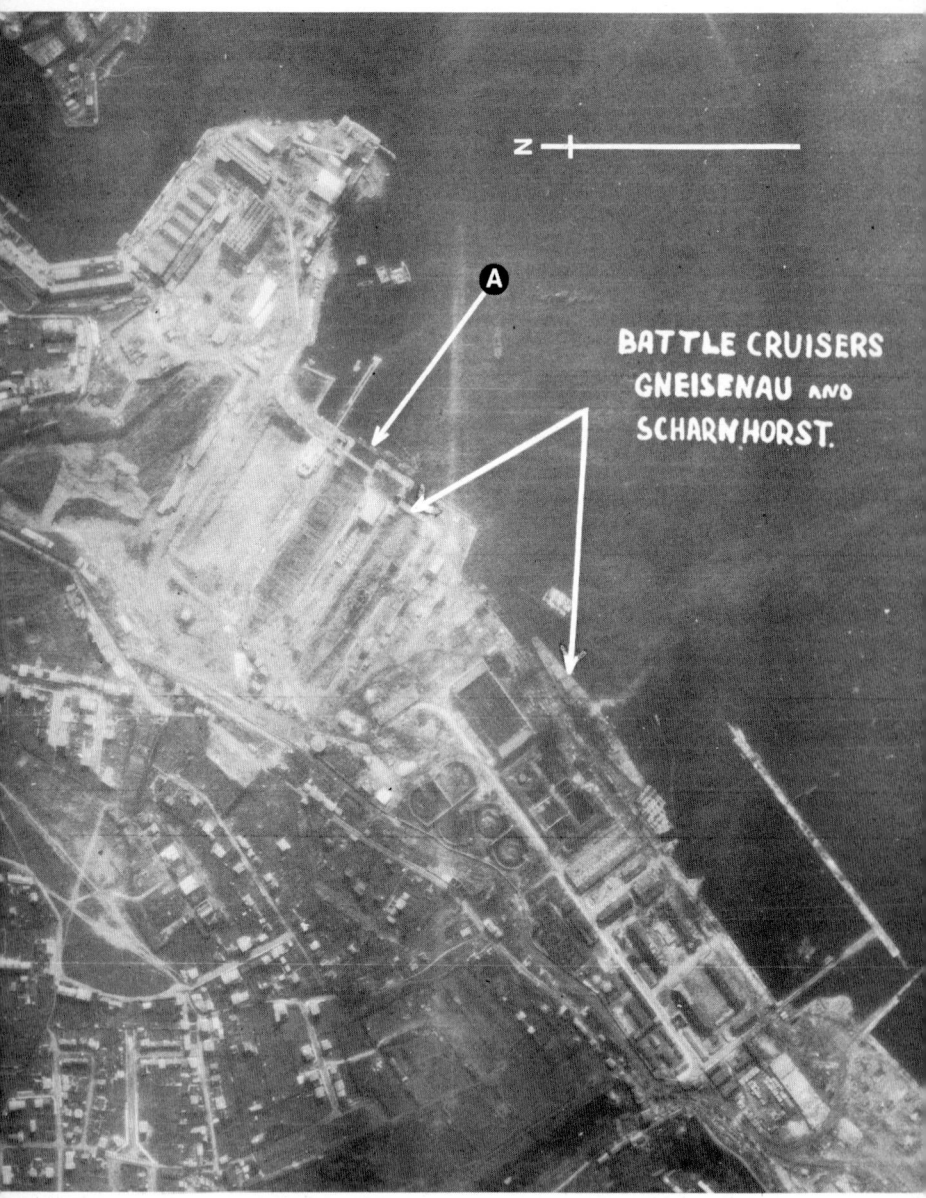

N |————————————

Ⓐ

BATTLE CRUISERS
GNEISENAU AND
SCHARNHORST.

Another part of Brest's harbour complex, photographed at the same time as
the preceding. The battle-cruisers are marked, *Gneisenau* having recently
been shifted from dry-dock 'A'; *Scharnhorst* is in a similar berth alongside,
and the picture is clouded by mist, indicating an early-morning sortie.

The reason for lack of detail in aerial photographs of *Prinz Eugen* at Brest: camouflage-netting covers every part of the ship's superstructure.

Vice-Admiral Otto Ciliax addresses the three ships' companies before their departure from Brest.

Messerschmitt 110 fighters which had provided the first aerial protection for some time after dawn before being replaced by single-seaters. They are seen here over part of the naval escort.

British radar at Dover was given special attention by the Nazis before the start of 'Operation Cerberus'. The clifftop masts are seen here through a telephoto lens on the French coast.

Opposite: In preparation for the escape, the armament of the capital ships was augmented with additional anti-aircraft guns. These are on the *Scharnhorst*.

Vice-Admiral Bertram Ramsay, Flag Officer, Dover, poses in the middle of his staff at the end of October 1941.

A lance-corporal and corporal of the ATS working as plotters on a table that requires them to lie on it, in Dover Castle.

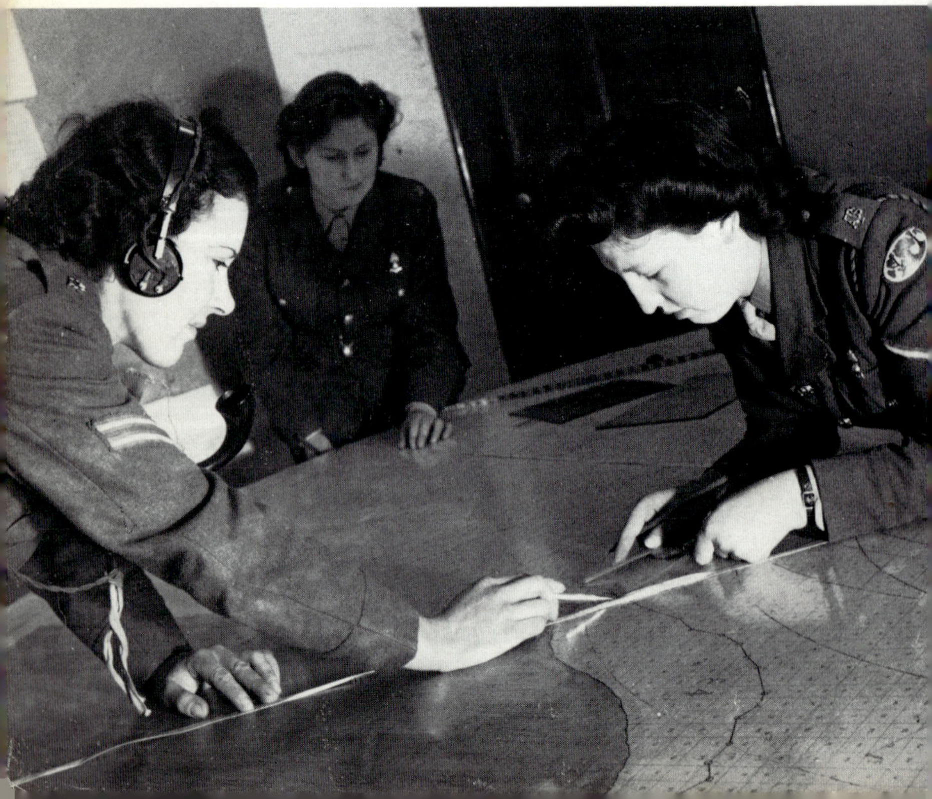

liked not at all the circular plots over a group of ships progressing at 25 knots. "An air-sea rescue operation," he was told. He shook his head and thought for a moment. "No convoy would move at that speed." With a grunt of finalization, he reached for his telephone and related his suspicions on the radar plots to No 11 Group Headquarters.

Security at Group could not have been better—indeed, it was too excellent, and none of those to whom he spoke had any knowledge of what he meant by 'Fuller'. As frustrated as the Flight-Lieutenant at Swingate had been, he rang the fighter station at Hawkinge, and it was his request that was to send the two 91 Squadron Spitfires off, with Squadron-Leader Oxspring and Sergeant Beaumont at the controls, to investigate and in the process to come near to accounting for the two from Kenley which they did not know were there.

At last things were moving, but only just, for a great deal of time had now been lost, and it was only at 10.43 p.m. that suspicions were voiced at Dover Headquarters. Admiral Ramsay and his air-liaison officer, Wing-Commander Constable-Roberts, decided that most probably the enemy had 'pulled a fast one' and broken out in daylight. One after the other the two officers reached for their telephones to start the chain of events that would begin efforts against an operation which they would be incapable of halting. The Vice-Admiral spoke briefly to the First Sea Lord. His face was set into a grim mask as he gave a single nod to his assistant to go ahead, and the Wing-Commander picked up his telephone and asked for Manston.

Although Eugene Esmonde's unit was at the base in Kent for just this contingency, he had been enjoying himself on the Wednesday because he had been summoned to London to receive the Distinguished Service Order from the hands of King George VI at Buckingham Palace. Now back at Manston, he was still in the process of licking into shape his semi-trained little group. Far more skilled and experienced than any of even its older members, he showed just the right mixture of fairness and discipline, applied with a light and understanding touch, to ensure their obedience and his popularity. When the voice at the other end of the telephone asked for him in person, he was out on the wind-swept airfield where the unit had been told to stand down until after dusk, so a runner had to be sent to fetch him.

A few minutes before, a Swordfish had just landed after a practice flight, and from the open cockpit Sub-Lieutenant Brian Rose and his observer had climbed stiffly down. They had divested themselves of their flying-clothing and were on the way to the mess when a lorry with others of the Squadron came tearing past, bumping and jolting over the grass as it did so. Someone in the back was shouting to them. Some of what was said they lost, but the operative words came over clearly enough: "The balloon's gone up!" The pair tore back to the crew-room and scrambled into their overalls again to join the rest of the group, including Charles Kingsmill who had dashed across half-way through having a hair-cut. Esmonde was already there and was immediately joined by the station-commander, Wing-Commander Tom Gleave. They all waited; the next telephone call would confirm or deny the suspicions which the RAF officer at Dover had already voiced. Then suddenly the silence was broken by the shrill ringing of the bell again. Esmonde picked up the receiver. At the other end was Constable-Roberts once more, and by the tone of his emotionless voice Esmonde must have realized that this was no denial.

Suddenly, ungainly, with the flaps and undercarriages down, the two Spitfires came in low over the snow-patched Surrey hills; for a moment the traditional guard-room block slipped beneath them, and then they were jolting over the airfield at Kenley on their stalky, narrow-track legs. It was exactly 11.09 a.m. when they taxied back and Group-Captain Beamish and Wing-Commander Boyd pushed back the hoods and clambered out.

Nineteen minutes earlier the two 91 Squadron Spitfires had landed back at Hawkinge, and what befell the four pilots afterwards is remarkably similar. Victor Beamish raced for the nearest telephone and did his level best to make a personal call to Trafford Leigh-Mallory; in this he was unsuccessful, as the Air Vice-Marshal was engaged in ceremonial duties at Northolt. Not far away, at Hawkinge, Bobby Oxspring was telling Sergeant Beaumont that he was sure the largest ship he had seen was either the *Scharnhorst* or the *Gneisenau*, although the rain had made identification difficult; a recognition-book of warships was sent for. Immediately after that, both Oxspring and the alert controller from Biggin Hill's operations room attempted to get the vital intelligence passed on to No 11 Group's AOC, but they fared no better than Beamish had done; 11 Group themselves remained sceptical.

Group Captain Beamish then decided on a final effort but only found himself talking for the third time to a staff officer to whom he refused to speak. Finally the Air Vice-Marshal's aide relented, and Northolt's tannoy crackled into life. The preliminary ceremonies before the presentation of Colours to the Belgian Air Force faltered for a moment as the metallic words requesting the AOC to report to the station headquarters rang out, and almost before they had been comprehended, an aide rushed across the parade-ground. The Guard of Honour was nearest to what followed, and they suspected a major crisis by the agitated gestures from the junior officer. A few minutes later all were certain of it, for the Air Vice-Marshal was in his car and was being driven at high speed to Group Headquarters at Uxbridge. But almost half an hour had been lost.

There are, even in what is commonly called 'the old school', two types of senior officer. On the one hand are those who are so completely democratic that the niceties of rank have but scant meaning to them except as parade courtesy, and frequently their enthusiasm for the service will mean that they can become involved in work and responsibilities beyond the demands of duty. There are some who do not remember No 11 Group's AOC as one of these, and it is certainly true to say that records do not report him as enjoying a benevolent mood when called to the telephone by a Group-Captain. Even so, Victor Beamish had tact and eloquence, and he used both now, adding that what he had seen was supported by others, so that his superior was eventually convinced. But by now about an hour had passed since Oxspring had blurted out his crudely worded alert.

In fact, the Nazi fleet had been keyed up for action long before this, since the warning had naturally been intercepted by their listening-service and all knew that at last the inevitable had happened and their run of luck was exhausted at last. But despite this state of affairs the enforced radio-silence was maintained without a break, while the spoof radar-signals were still sent out by the Heinkel patrols, and the jamming from the direction of the French coast persisted.

It was now almost midday, and the squadron of ships, having reached its most formidable strength, was entering the narrowest part of the Channel, having completed about two-thirds of the journey. By now the aerial umbrella was composed entirely of single-seat day fighters, the last of the night machines having left an hour earlier. They had done their work well, but now it was time to relax at their Dutch bases before being required again as the evening closed in.

Eighteen miles to port lay the cliffs of Dover, invisible in the murk as the cloud-base dropped lower, yet, perhaps as much for psychological reasons as anything else, the order was given to the vessels on that side to make smoke. At any other time the head of the concealing blanket would have marked their position to long-range artillery, but now it would act as a cover against any marauding Royal Navy warship that suddenly loomed through the fog.

In fact no one as yet had a completely accurate idea of the squadron's position as reported by the Spitfire pilots—somewhere "off Boulogne".

At sea, the armada of ships still ploughed on. The weather was poorer now, with seven-tenths cloud and deteriorating, and with visibility around 1,400 yards. It remained cold, no more than 41 degrees Fahrenheit, so that the hot coffee served to the officers on watch at their exposed forward positions was doubly welcome. The extra E-boats had now met their charges, and together all made good progress, the crews mentally congratulating themselves on the incredible luck. But by noon it was only too easy to see that the weather had taken a determined turn for the worst as the slight but persistent rain came from a cloud-base now no more than 900 and at times only 600 feet above sea level.

Such a state of affairs was another piece of good fortune, for, had the squadron been discovered earlier so that the fighter escort had been forced to exhaust itself at the Channel's more easterly end, the pilots would now be no longer fresh and alert. As we have already seen, although there were some reinforcements, they were slight, for (as the Intelligence Section at RAF Fighter Headquarters was to comment quite correctly at a later date) with the exception of the routine flights, such as Zenit and reconnaissance sorties, the safety of the capital ships had taken up virtually the whole of the Nazi Luftwaffe's effort in France and the Low Countries. In addition to the fighter units already described, plus the contribution from the bombers, the experienced anti-shipping units KGr106 and 3/122 had been transferred to Eindhoven from respectively Dinard and Montdidier on only the previous day, a measure taken to indicate that the heaviest opposition would not be encountered until the Straits of Dover were reached.

In fact, the plans drawn up by the Luftwaffe were extremely thorough and went far beyond the actual demands of providing a protective escort for the ships and included attacks carried out by bombers on the aerodromes at Exeter and Warmwell, the former station being one commonly associated with the offensive against shipping in the North Sea and English Channel that was conducted by No 2 Group, the latter being a fighter station from which the Canadian No 402 Squadron flew Hurricanes. It seems likely that these raids were carried out by III/KG2, which had certainly been moved on 8th February from Eindhoven to Evreux. At first sight it may be obscure why sorties of this nature had any connection with the larger operation being carried out in the Channel, particularly when they occurred at a time when the vessels were still some distance from the neighbourhood of Cherbourg, but it was hoped that these operations would be misconstrued by the RAF as indicating that the movement of the capital ships was contemplated but had not yet begun. In an attempt to confuse the picture further, the smoke-screen that had served so well at Brest the night before was maintained for the entire day after the warships had left.

More obviously connected with the larger mission was the work of the reconnaissance units who were charged with maintaining a watch on the movements of British naval forces. Patrols were spread over a considerable area, from the Wash to Texel, covering the North Sea and as far east as a line from Dunkirk to North Foreland. Indeed, the day was to see the highest number of reconnaissance sorties flown that year, amounting to eighty in all, of which only seven were directed to cover the mainland.

Now, as the Nazi squadron continued on its way, all was still peaceful and the quiet that reigned was broken only by the slap of the water against the ship's sides. All the men could do was to wait, with collars turned up against the cold, for the storm to break. Some became uneasy and suspected a trap of some sort; they could only eye the British coastline through the occasional gaps in the low cloud where, with the aid of glasses, it was possible to pick out the barrage-balloons above the cliffs, but even this diversion was denied to those on the three major vessels cocooned in the enveloping smoke laid by the attendant destroyers.

There was no atmosphere of such quietude among the British however. 'Fuller' had burst unheralded and during daylight, taking everyone by surprise. Ace in the pack which the Royal Navy had to play in the desperate game was the little flight of Swordfish aircraft commanded by Eugene Esmonde, and now the sturdy biplanes were being loaded with their torpedoes 'set deep'. The leader was anxious to be away, as there was a strong likelihood of the fleet having passed from the most favourable point for an attack before contact could be made if too much time was lost, but it was essential, he was told, to wait until proper fighter protection could be arranged; there was no intention that this was to be a suicide mission.

Ten minutes were taken to complete the details, involving five squadrons in all. Of these, three were to form the close cover, and the remaining pair were to go in to sweep the decks of the flak-ships immediately ahead of the torpedo-bombers; Biggin Hill was to find the first of these, and the strafing was to be done by the Hornchurch Spitfires. All that could be done in the time had by now been carried out, and it seemed on the surface that there was at least a fifty-fifty chance of survival for some of the Swordfish. But the better-informed, including Esmonde (the usually cheery young man who in happier days would answer inexplicably to the nickname of "Winkle"), were not deceived. In the last moments, while flying-clothing was pulled on by the eighteen men and while they waited until the latest speed, course and position of the armada (as far as it was known) was transmitted, those who knew Esmonde best were staggered by the alteration in his appearance. Now his face was almost haggard, the colour gone and a death-like glaze covering his eyes. Inwardly he and his flight must have realized that they were doomed, but training overcomes emotion, and they went from the crew-room door to where the Swordfish waited, armed, fuelled and with engines warm. Esmonde was the last to go, and at the final moment the overworked telephone rang once again. The call was from Fighter Command's No 11 Group, and the message could now do no more than confirm the sentence that had been passed. The fighters would be a little late.

There were those who afterwards said that, pausing in the doorway, the devout Esmonde quoted the last words of a six-teenth-century martyr uttered on his way to execution.

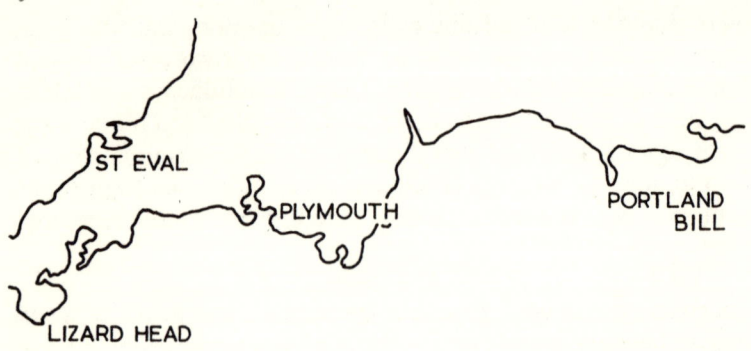

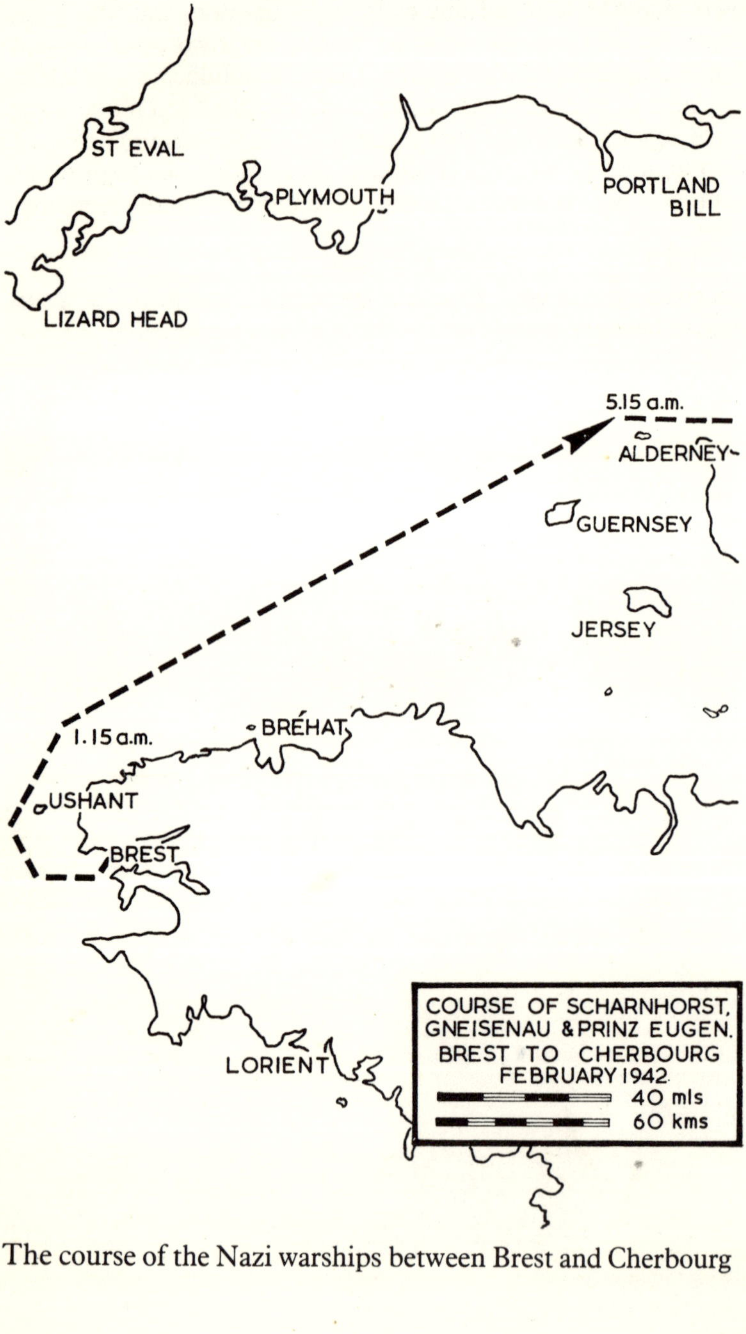

ST EVAL

PLYMOUTH

PORTLAND
BILL

LIZARD HEAD

5.15 a.m.

ALDERNEY

GUERNSEY

JERSEY

1.15 a.m.

BRÉHAT

USHANT

BREST

LORIENT

COURSE OF SCHARNHORST,
GNEISENAU & PRINZ EUGEN.
BREST TO CHERBOURG
FEBRUARY 1942.
40 mls
60 kms

The course of the Nazi warships between Brest and Cherbourg

5

At All Costs

The eighteen young Royal Navy men who made up the crews of the Swordfish aircraft required one final piece in the jig-saw of information that would send them bumping over Manston's frozen grass towards their fate: the exact position of the enemy squadron. It was not long in coming, for, despite the element of surprise and the general atmosphere of disbelief that had frustrated speedier action and lost more valuable time, certain elements of the navy had done their best to remedy matters in some measure, and even at that moment five motor torpedo-boats were racing towards the last known position of the audacious armada.

The flotilla under the command of Lieutenant-Commander E.N. Pumphrey was a little over 5 miles from its quarry but was unable to sight them in the poor visibility and through the smoke-screen. Still they dashed on, and then, quite suddenly, through a gap in the protective smoke, there they were, behind a defensive screen of E-boats, the "three great ships", as Pumphrey was to describe them later, "which frightened us quite a lot".

Previous to this, only the vaguest idea of the position of the enemy vessels was known, and when the MTBs had "got the buzz to get cracking shortly after lunch", before they went down to their boats "in a terrific rush", Lieutenant A.E. Fanning, the first MTB's gunnery officer, had received no more exact briefing than to expect the Nazis beyond mid-Channel. Final indication of the position had been established by the two great clouds of smoke. Now, to give time for the 'enemy sighted' signal to be sent back to Dover, together with an accurate estimate of the course, position and speed of the flotilla, the MTBs did not immediately close in but turned and made their way parallel to the outer screen, where, at least for the moment, they excited little reaction from the patrolling vessels. Not so among the Luftwaffe, however, for the protecting fighters "came buzzing all around". The British gunners at once opened up, and a running fight ensured of small surface vessels versus Nazi fighters, with Messerschmitt 109s predominating. During a subsequent interview, Lieutenant-Commander Pumphrey was to be quoted as saying, "We recognized the *Prinz Eugen*, and it was only then that we realized what we were after."

Yet for Admiral Ciliax there was no real confirmation that the enemy knew exactly his position, and he was enjoying a period of comparative calm in his flagship, where he stood on the bridge sipping hot coffee and huddled in his thick naval great-coat above which the scarf wound about his throat would have provided a sharp contrast to any British eyes (could they but have seen him) with the summery look given by the white-topped cap at that time donned by the Royal Navy only between May and October.

As the hands of the clock crept to 12.19 p.m., there came from the port beam a crash and a roar, at the same moment sending up a great column of water. There was no call to enquire from whence it came (all on board the three capital ships knew that the successful negotiation of the minefield laid by HMS *Plover* was but the first of their problems). Now the long-range guns had opened up, and as the fleet drew abreast of the positions manned by the 540th Regiment of Artillery on top of Dover's cliffs, the ships were a sitting (if, thanks to the foul weather, invisible) target. The guns that had just fired their first half-salvo as a ranging-shot had not long been in position and were consequently untried, having not yet fired their initial practice-series.

Guns in position at the time of the rush up the English Channel by the Nazi vessels were of several types, not all of them suitable for shooting at a surface vessel several miles out to sea but better at the land targets some 22 miles distant, and the array of artillery was in the process of being augmented by the 15-inch guns of the Wanstone Battery then being installed. Of the others there were, of course, the railguns of 13·5 inch calibre and the 18-inch 'Boche-Buster' howitzer used from the track of the Elham Valley Light Railway; these monsters contrasted with the small Mark XXIV guns of 6-inch calibre concealed in their casements at Fan Bay and Langdon and the similar ones in the open emplacements at Lydden Spout. Whatever their type, the majority of the others were unsuitable for engaging shipping targets close to the French shore because either they were of insufficient range or they were too slow to allow their being brought to bear on vessels moving at such speed.

The guns which fired the first shots in the attempt to prevent the escape of the Nazi capital ships were therefore the quartet of the South Foreland Battery situated high up on Dover's cliffs, some 350 feet above sea level, under the lea of Summerhouse Hill, They were of the Mark X variety and were the updated version of a long family of 9·2-inch guns that had begun as far back as 1894 and in its latest form was capable of hurling a shell weighing 380 pounds over a distance of 31,300 yards, although this range was later extended by a further 4,700 yards.

This battery had been ready for action since May of the previous year, and it now seemed that, with the Nazi warships so close at hand, its most spectacular success was about to take place. This likelihood seemed to be increased because of the guns' linkage to an early radar system by means of which it was possible, as ex-accountant Brigadier Cecil Raw, the Coastal Artillery Commander was later to claim, to maintain a watch on any of the French ports between and even beyond Cherbourg in one direction and Ostend in the other, while any ship-movement either to the north or southwards towards Boulogne or Calais could be similarly tracked. Advance information of this nature was transmitted to particular radar-operators who would then observe a specific area, and it therefore followed that the course of any flotilla or even of individual vessels could be plotted on the main table dominating the centre of the Dover operations room, along with the estimated strength and number of ships; data, such as this with the speed of the vessels, was immediately sent to the gun-sites where the Fire-Commanders would be waiting to engage the unseen targets. However, this was a more difficult than may at first be supposed, for maritime formations could alter their speed, position and course, and the only means by which these alterations could be tracked was from study of the blips of a flickering cathode-ray tube. The recognition of these called for their interpretation by experienced operators, but a largely accurate idea of what could be expected was possible if the situation were viewed in the light of intercepted enemy radio-messages.

When the half salvo had exploded in the water off the port beam of the vessels now groping their way up the Channel, it had marked not only the first offensive action against the Nazi ships but also the opening of the very first action to be fought by coastal artillery acting under radar control, happily equipped with sets of K-type in view of the jamming of the older M-sets that was still being carried out by the enemy.

The conditions under which the action took place were such as to make impossible any form of bombardment without electronic aid, for although the snow that had lain on the ground for over a week had by now largely vanished locally in a quick over-night thaw two days before, it had left behind weather that was cold, damp and foggy. However, at the time fire was opened visibility from the shore was a few thousand yards, clearing intermittently to allow a glimpse of the ships, and a little later the Brigadier, who had certain misgivings of the ability of his 9·2-inch guns to engage them at such range, was to repair to the Castle look-out point to attempt to see the target at first hand with the aid of a pair of captured Italian binoculars.

It had been 11.20 a.m. when the first intimation of the approaching flotilla had been received in the Dover operations room, and ten minutes were to elapse before the first radar reports were received. These came from a newly installed set at K148, situated between Dover and Folkestone, the estimated range being 46,000 yards—26 miles, at a bearing of 166 degrees. Although much has been said about the degree of non-co-operation between the Services at this time, it was by no means total, for only one minute later came confirmation of the radar plot from the Royal Navy, which added that twenty-five other vessels were currently escorting the capital ships and that the speed of the group was in the region of 25 knots.

Immediately on the receipt of this confirmation the Battery Commander was warned to prepare for action. Unfortunately the roaring of the Klaxon was greeted with some incredulity at the site, and the gun-drill then in progress was allowed to continue by a duty officer who telephoned his commander to question the order.

By now midday was approaching, and at 11.50 a.m. the results of K148's continued tracking of the target began to be passed on to the South Foreland Battery. Meanwhile, in the operations room, now a hive of activity, Admiral Ramsay strode impatiently between the large map displays with a couple of bulldogs at his heels; at one point he was observed to nod, almost to himself, as his mind was made up, before going across to where Raw was sitting above the main table. Placing his hand on the Brigadier's shoulder, he murmured, "Engage when ready."

By now the hand on the colourful ops room clock had crept to three minutes past noon, and the radar reports continued to flow in. Now the leading battle-cruiser with Admiral Ciliax on the bridge was 32,000 yards—18 miles—from the South Foreland Battery and maintaining speed. The fire-control post was able to report at the same instant, "Ready for action."

While this was going on, the NT284 radar set had been acting as the battery range-finder and, since it had not yet been able to pick up the target fire, had to be withheld. A pregnant three minutes passed, and then, in the gloom of the radar-operators' cubicle, a small blip appeared on the restless green scan. The operators knew that this was what they had been seeking and bent the more closely over their tubes. They swung their servos and watched. There was no question now: they were following the flotilla out there behind the smoke in the mist-shrouded Channel. At 12.19 p.m. the long-awaited order rang out on the cold air, "Fire!", and with a roar and a belch of acrid smoke the first half-salvo tore towards the unseen target—a mixed blessing this because the radar sets were incapable of registering where the shells were falling, and the weather effectively prevented any visual 'fall of shot' observation.

This state of affairs was one that existed not for the want of trying to overcome it, however, and the men crouched at the NT284 set did their best to see something that would indicate on their screens some clue of the accuracy of fire. At 12.23 p.m. another half-salvo was fired, and again the radar was unsuccessful in observing the fall. Almost the next moment they lost contact with the enemy ships completely, and it was almost five minutes, while the operators worked at the crude pioneer sets, before it was found again.

With the range-finding set restored, it was decided to fire a third half-salvo, loosed at exactly 12.28 p.m., but this too fell unobserved. During this, the target was tending to steam away at speed, and so orders went out from the operations room for no further 'fall of shot' observations to be waited for but for fire to be resumed with four-gun salvos. One minute later the first of these sent up a massive four-pronged fork of water as the shells exploded some distance to the port side of the Nazi squadron, and immediately afterwards the order was given for a second full-salvo, which was fired precisely on the half-hour.

There was still to hand no observation of the fall, and subsequently it was ordered that an extra 1,000 yards be added to the range. The first of these shots was fired one minute later. Just at that moment the message was delivered that NT284 had in fact been successful in observing the results of the salvo fired on the half-hour and that it appeared to have fallen some 2,000 yards short of the target. In the light of this, and in view of the fact that the range had already been extended, that fired at 12.32 p.m. had a further 1,000 yards added.

Although, as we now know, this was still short of the flotilla by some distance, it seems that it was this salvo which triggered off some consternation in Nazi mess circles, for the word quickly went round that a hit had been scored on, it was generally agreed, the *Prinz Eugen*. JG52, grounded on Jever airfield throughout the operations of 12th February on account of the weather, added for good measure the unfounded intelligence that extensive damage had been caused. In fact, all this was pure speculation, but the matter had its counterpart in the Dover operations room where the NT284 set recorded a hit on the target, or at least a near miss.

Even at this distance in time exactly what took place is unclear, because shooting under conditions such as those which were prevailing presented enormous odds against a hit on the target. Even so, although at no time were the possible additional explosions heard that would have certainly indicated a hit, the British radar certainly registered a sudden alteration of course, and an RAF pilot among the force which was sent to bomb the capital ships came back with ecstatic reports of not one but a seeming total of four shells hitting the vessels.

The roar of another whole-salvo was heard again only moments later, and this was surprisingly accompanied by the sound of additional explosions. Yet these came not from the hoped-for direction of the sea but from the land near to the gun emplacements and were in fact the first indication that the Nazi guns on the coast of France were returning fire in defence of the warships in the Channel. The exact source of the reply from the enemy guns was difficult to assess, since then visibility was beginning to deteriorate once more, but from time to time the murk lifted so that the battery observation-post on the cliffs below the lighthouse was able to obtain a glimpse of the armada.

In addition to the normal camouflage that was set up to protect British and Nazi emplacements alike, the methods of providing decoys against observation varied between the two sides. Whereas the Dover batteries were in the main hidden by extensive netting, clearly visible near-to but providing good camouflage at any distance, flash-boxes were set up on the French coast amongst the real guns, and these decoys were of similar intensity to a genuine muzzle-flash and synchronized with the discharge of the authentic article. British attempts to hide the position of the long-range guns were less elaborate and, apart from camouflage along the lines already described, were made up mainly of dummy guns intended primarily to confuse the issue for aerial reconnaissance.

Whatever the value of these, it was certainly small now, and the fire from France was fairly accurate. Several shells landed in the vicinity of the South Foreland Battery and its fire-control post, although no damage was caused nor was the rate of fire from the British gunners interrupted, so that two full-salvos were fired at 12.33 and 12.34 p.m., exactly one minute before another Nazi salvo exploded nearby.

The South Foreland guns were now firing at a range of 30,000 yards—17 miles, and at 12.36 p.m. another salvo was loosed off, aimed at the believed leading *Scharnhorst* with the aid of NT284. However, this radar-post had been unable to keep track of the fall of the last three shots and could no longer monitor the course of the first vessel, so the order to cease fire was given. Immediately upon this, the Fire-Commander received orders to attempt to pick up the two further ships in the main group. Although the NT284 set failed to do this, the K-set succeeded in following the first target to a range of 65,000 yards as it moved steadily away. The reason for the inability to find the further vessels was that in the confusion it had been the capital ship at the end of the line, the *Prinz Eugen*, which had in fact been the target, so there were no further vessels behind to track. Therefore, despite the continued radar observation of this ship, it was no part of the duties of the K-set to provide range-finding facilities or to make 'fall of shot' observations. Thus, when the air seemed to shake and the earth tremble once more with the discharge of another salvo at 12.36 p.m., this was the last firing of the South Foreland 9·2s, and afterwards they were silent.

Not so, however, their Nazi counterparts, for with the rushing sound that the people of Dover were now becoming familiar with a crash and a roar told that two more salvos were aimed from the French coast at 12.50 p.m., followed by another two minutes later. Like the others, they did no more than explode harmlessly in the chalky farmland nearby.

This had been the first action of coastal artillery against vessels passing through the Dover Straits, and the use of radar had made it an historic one since fire-control along those lines had not been tried out before. It had lasted for only seventeen minutes, due to the speed of the target, but in that space of time thirty-three rounds had been fired, including the believed hits. But it had all been to no avail, since, in the words of Brigadier Raw, "The targets, protected as they were by their heavy armour and helped by their high speed, were neither sunk nor halted."

The majority of the remaining Dover guns had been silent during the passage of the three ships, and there were many expressions of regret that the 15-inch guns of Wanstone Battery were not yet ready to play a part. At the time this pair of monsters, capable of firing a 1,938-pound shell over nearly 24 miles, were being installed at Wanstone Farm close by St Margaret's at Cliffe, almost due north of Bantam Hole and not far from the South Foreland Battery which they were first to support in August of the same year.

The four 9·2s above the lighthouse were not the only pieces of coastal artillery to engage the *Scharnhorst*, *Gneisenau* and *Prinz Eugen* on that cold and fateful February day, although the fact that this is so has now been largely forgotten. In addition there was a 14-inch gun whose installation may be traced directly back to a meeting called in June 1940 by Winston Churchill, who insisted on some form of protection for the British convoys which, he demanded with splendid insolence, should continue to sail up the Channel under the very noses of the occupation forces in France. The outcome of this had been another conference, but this time between the gun-design team from Vickers-Armstrong and the Director of Ordnance. Weapons decided on were to be ex-naval Mark 7 guns of 14-inch calibre that had at first been destined for battleships of the *King George V* Class; since these vessels were still incomplete, four barrels were released, and the first was to be set on modified mountings designed for 18-inch naval guns.

Moved by the spirit of urgency that typified the time, it was only the end of the same June when the first of these began its journey to Dover. Due to the size and weight of the barrel alone, this posed several problems, and an idea of the magnitude of the task of transporting an item of such weight may be formed from the fact that these guns were designed to fire a shell of 1,400-pounds over a range of 47,200 yards (that is, the best part of 28 miles), so that a gun in the region of 100 tons in weight was necessary. Transporting such a bulky item was further complicated by the great length of the barrel. However, all these tasks were swiftly and efficiently dealt with by the Southern Railway, the forerunner of today's Southern Region of British Rail.

Having delivered the gun to its destination, the next problem was the moving of so large an item through the town, and this provided a prolonged spectacle for the inhabitants, who witnessed it being slowly manœuvred through the narrow streets and then up the gradient of Castle Hill where the site had been prepared ready for the installation on 13th July by men of the Royal Marine Siege Regiment, who had received their training at Catterick. Not long after, 'A' Battery, as it was officially known, began to be dubbed 'Winnie' after the Prime Minister who had 'fathered' the idea, so that it was only a short step, calling for a strange mental reconciliation between the nickname for Winston Churchill and A.A. Milne's character, to name the second gun of the same type 'Pooh', erstwise 'B' Battery, when this took up its position in February 1941.

The problems for 'A' Battery were not by any means over. In order to achieve the required range, more powerful charges were from the first utilized, but these had the drawback of imposing a great strain on the barrels, so that they had to be replaced at more frequent intervals than was anticipated. Fifty rounds were enough to effect the rifling sufficiently to call for their replacement, and this point was reached by 'Winnie' in the first six months of use. Other problems were also encountered, and one of a major nature was to be found in the question of aiming. This is a reference not to the small traverse of both 'A' and 'B' Battery but to the difficulties encountered by the gun layers. The root of this problem was to be found in the use of ordnance maps and sea charts which, despite constant revision, were not aligned to give the correct relationship between the French and English coasts. In order to set matters to rights once and for all, the task of correcting this was undertaken by Captain W. E. Brown of the Royal Engineers, who plotted the position of 'Winnie', on the former golf-course high above St Margaret's Bay, in relation to the French coast, so that, as he was afterwards humorously to claim, he had "succeeded in getting England and France in correct relation geographically for the first time in history".

The question of the worn barrels was not so simply solved, however, and the two guns were maintained increasingly on a 'care and maintenance' basis—in effect waiting for some major future undertaking: for 'Winnie' and 'Pooh' that day seemed to have arrived on 12th February 1942, when the Nazi capital ships appeared in the Channel.

Capricious fate seemed to have taken a hand in matters here, although this is really a euphemism for lack of preparedness and foresight, for the crews of both 'Winnie' and 'Pooh' were away on a training-exercise and had to be ordered back in some haste—a classic illustration of the lack of co-ordination between the Services, for, as we have seen in an earlier chapter, Coastal Command's Air Officer Commanding in Chief had already issued what amounted to a written warning that the state of the probable weather, the phase of the moon and the preparedness of the Nazi vessels all augured for a break-out in that period.

This was not all, and the flurry of activity included the issuing of orders that either 'Sceneshifter' or 'Piecemaker', the 13·5-inch railway guns, be moved from Guston to Martin Mill and prepared for action.

It took a little time for the men to be returned to the site at St Margaret's occupied by the 14-inch Mark VIIs, but this was accomplished with as great a despatch as possible, and 1 and 2 Troops of the Royal Marine Siege Regiment's 'A' Battery were ordered to stand by. The reports that reached them during this time did nothing to clarify the situation. One of the strangest was that which declared that the radar a little east of Hastings was at that moment tracking the movement of the ships after first registering their appearance at a record distance of 67,000 yards—in fact the Fairlight cathode-ray tubes were blank, as the sets had chosen that moment to break down, although this was in no way due to the Nazi jamming since Fairlight, like Foreness and Dover, was a CHL (Chain Home Low) station with a rotating aerial which put it in the 'new' category of the time.

It was now 12.30 p.m., and although the roar of the South Foreland guns could be clearly heard, no order for the Marines to open fire had been received. Now the commander decided to take action, and the 14-inch guns were ordered to fire one round each. Just what this was expected to achieve is difficult to speculate, since the target could not be seen, and there was no way of observing the results of the shot-fall. Range was set on a predetermined position at 30,000 yards, and the order to fire was given. The results were inevitable and dismal: two fountains of water to the port side of the flotilla and then nothing more. It only gave the batteries on the French coast a chance to set a more accurate range, and it was only a short time before the shells arrived from the Naval Coast Battalion on Cap Gris Nez. With this futile show of aggression and the more determined effort from the South Foreland Battery, the contribution of the coastal artillery to the battle of the narrow sea was over.

However, as with so much else connected with the whole fiasco that was the attempt to engage the Nazi flotilla conclusively, one wonders how much it contributed to the subsequent march of events.

It has been stated that preparatory work was already under way for the setting-up of a new battery of long-distance guns at Wanstone Farm, and it seems that this took on a new urgency, for the first of the pair of 15-inch weapons was ready for use during the following month. (J, K and L Troops of the 540th

Coast Regiment of the RA quickly dubbed it 'Jane' after the shapely young lady in the *Daily Mirror* cartoon who always lost her garments at awkward moments.) There were concrete paths to each gun, and light tractors were to be used to draw the ammunition to the monster breaches. Earlier readiness might have resulted in a different conclusion to the saga of the guns, but the truth is still shrouded in mystery, for there were reports claiming that the *Friedrich Ihn* had at one time deliberately drawn the fire of the artillery to save the *Prinz Eugen*.

All these British measures were controlled from the nerve-centre that lay at the focal-point of the labyrinth that was Dover Castle, an ancient monument dating from Norman times situated on the highest point overlooking the harbour. The crews of the operations rooms were quartered there as well as doing their spells of duty within the massive walls, so that it was possible for them to be incarcerated under the artificial lighting for perhaps a week.

In fact, there were two rooms, one for the Army and the other to direct naval operations, and these were distinctly separate—so much so in fact that a long walk through the passages divided them. The scope for communication was therefore poor since direct telephone linkage (which crews in the years to come were to regard as normal) was conspicuously absent, and what dealings one had with the other had to be handled entirely by the naval signals office, with an inevitable delay. With the towering masts on Swingate Downs above (not far from the spot where Louis Blériot had landed after his cross-Channel flight thirty-three years before—nearer in time than we are to the escape of the Nazi warships), the main artery of information for the plotting-tables was supplied by radar, although even this was done from the local source by rather round-about circulation, since this radar station, being an RAF establishment, had no direct contact with, say, the guns commanded by Cecil Raw.

Despite this form of inter-Service isolationism, there still remained sufficient information being fed in at three-minute intervals to keep a fairly accurate picture of the progress of events, although, as we have already seen, the Nazi jamming had taken quite a serious toll of the only radar system of which they were aware. The manner of doing this had been extremely subtle, for it had been introduced gradually over a period of time. The day before the ships had finally made their escape Colonel B. E. Wallace, who commanded the Home Forces' Army Signals Interception Unit, whose job it was to monitor Nazi radio traffic, had complained about this jamming to Dr R. V. Jones, the Scientific Intelligence Officer. At first it had been only slight, but over the days it had been slowly increased, with the result that its intensity was not wholly realized, and it had tended to become accepted. Although this interference had been reported, little notice had been taken, so carefully had the problem been brought in.

The world within an operations room is a particularly cloistered one, entirely shut off as it is from every-day activity, and one emerges from it with a feeling of surprise that any other form of life exists. On this day the atmosphere was heightened by the weather which could be here and there glimpsed through the few windows that gave onto the outside world, but if the tension within was great, with few if any of the plotters knowing just what it was they were tracking, those feelings were all the greater on the English coast.

After the sound of the exchange of fire between the heavy artillery had died away, the comparative quiet permitted the other noises of battle to be plainly heard, coming in from the narrow sea, announcing that the MTBs from Ramsgate and the MGBs based on Dover, plus the torpedo-boats from that port, had found the enemy. The sounds of battle thus wafting in gave to some the idea that an invasion was actually being attempted, and so strong was the impression on the minds of some that in the days to follow some newspapers published 'artists' impressions' of violent air battles actually being fought out over the Castle itself—a strange contrast with such peaceful items as the cinema advertisements for *Hoppity Goes to Town*, *Dumbo*, and Tyrone Power, Rita Hayworth and Linda Darnell in *Blood and Sand*, repeating the original Valentino success of twenty years before, or, here allowing the admission that there was in fact a war on, James Cagney as the *Captain of the Clouds*.

This certainty that an invasion was actually taking place even led to stories that the church bells had been rung in some areas, for during the war years the peals of places of worship were silent unless warning had to be given of an imminent invasion. So fixed was the idea in the minds of some that three days later a

Sunday newspaper was reporting the remarks alleged to have
been made by Lieutenant-Colonel Madden who had earned
himself a Military Cross for gallantry in the earlier conflict. At a
British Legion Conference he is supposed to have commented
on the signal from the church towers (although like the good
soldier he was he added that he only "understood" the alle-
gation), saying "I cannot tell where it was, but obviously it was
somewhere on the English coast opposite Brest." Questioned
on this point by a reporter, it fell to the War Office coldly to put
the matter to rights with, "We have no reports of bells being
rung."

Some stories there were of an even wilder nature, although
the wartime Englishman was always possessed of a marble calm
that was the envy of others. Perhaps the prize for the best tale
should go to the originator of the one that told of the Nazi
warships tying up at Brighton's Palace Pier for drinks before
proceeding!

6

Enemy Sighted

An atmosphere of calm had descended on the naval base at Dover by 11th February. In contrast to the warning that had already been issued by Air Chief Marshal Sir Philip Joubert about the favourability of the prevailing weather for a break from Brest, it was generally regarded that the emergency had passed. Indeed, so deep was the official conviction of this that the details of the proposed 'Operation Fuller', albeit intended to deal with a rush up the Channel under cover of darkness, were even now firmly locked in a safe, and the only officer who knew the whereabouts of the key was away on leave. Despite this chaotic state of affairs, something had to be done to improvise, and as midday approached, the first of the sea-borne attempts to destroy the capital ships were getting started, for although even then the Dover guns were under orders to open fire, their handicaps were realized.

It was exactly 11.55 a.m. when Lieutenant-Commander Nigel Pumphrey's five MTBs finally left. They had passed most of the morning at torpedo-practice and had been forced to waste valuable time exchanging the harmless torpedoes for live ones, and the little group represented the only five craft of the type that Dover could muster in serviceable condition.

The enemy had been sighted at first by the look-out on Pumphrey's leading *221*, a boat substituted for his usual *38*, which was in dry-dock. Behind raced Mark Arnold-Foster's *219*, followed by *45* commanded by Hilary Gamble, slightly older than the others and already decorated with a Distinguished Service Cross. The cold oil in the engines caused them to emit a strange, rough note, but the practised ear could make out that this was not the reason for the odd sound coming from the next in line, *44*, in the charge of Australian Dick

Saunders. Behind came *48*, another MTB commanded by an overseas officer, this time a Canadian, Tony Law.

Now, as the flotilla raced alongside the enemy vessels, they realized that they were slowly losing their quarry, for they could reach only 27 knots, and the Nazi ships were exceeding this by an extra three. Clearly too, with a flotilla effectively reduced to four boats, there was no chance of closing the range, so Pumphrey, now also plagued by a faulty engine, ordered that individual attacks be carried out and at the same time that his own vessel reduce speed. This enabled him to hold off while the Nazi squadron passed by, until one of the prime targets came abreast of him. But this also meant that *221* became something of a 'sitting duck' for the E-boats and fighters above. The gunners "gave them a terrific burst", but the surface vessels were ignored, for at that moment at only 4,000 yards range what was in fact the *Scharnhorst* seemed to fill the Englishmen's vision.

On the battle-cruiser all this was plainly visible even to the movement of the commander's hand as it struck down on the firing-lever, sending a pair of torpedoes leaping from the deck. There was no hit, and after a moment's pause Pumphrey's boat swung away and "belted off"; at the same time a great roar burst upon their hearing as a huge fountain of water was flung up. For a moment the men looked at each other questioningly. There was no reason for rejoicing: it was just one of the radar-controlled shots from Dover's South Foreland Battery.

Much the same is also true of three of the following MTBs. They waited for a target and slammed down on their firing-triggers, although both *219* and *48* had gone through some nasty moments to achieve their position, braving fire from both E-boats and fighters to reach them. Together with Gamble's *45*, they all retired to see their torpedoes miss and sink before the E-boats closed in afresh, *45* receiving the largest share of the attention as it was the last to deliver its attack. With great skill the German seamen had presented as small a target as possible by turning their large vessels through as much as ninety degrees in some cases so that the single torpedo failed to find its mark, the second not getting away.

Now the MTBs were in real trouble, for the E-boats had given way to something larger, the destroyer *Friedrich Ihn,* which towered over the little British boats, and once more the rearmost MTB was having the worst of it. In the choppy sea and dreadful visibility the *Friedrich Ihn*'s fire was inaccurate, but things looked grim for the smaller craft, for now that their torpedoes were gone, they had little by which to defend themselves save their rifle-calibre machine-guns. At that moment they must have wished that they carried something like the 20-millimetre guns of the E-boats or that the others of their number which had been ordered from Dover only the previous day might still be present.

The legend runs that at this point a trick saved the day—a feint depth-charge attack, although the British boats were in fact not thus armed. Whatever the truth of the matter, something certainly caused the Nazi destroyer to alter course suddenly, and although this offered only momentary relief, it was long enough for the MTBs to take advantage of the local conditions. These took the form of two hazards, one man-made—a partially cleared minefield, the other natural—submerged sandbanks, and it was towards the latter, which offered insufficient depth for a vesel of a destroyer's draft, that the fugitives now raced.

Meanwhile, Saunders' No *44* had recovered from her recalcitrant engine and had joined the fight. The Australian sized up the situation at a glance. The E-boats were still there, but now they were strung out in a line like hounds after a good fox. With a spin of the wheel, *44* slipped in aft of the final Nazi craft so that it was no more than 3,000 yards from the last of the capital ships at which the torpedoes were loosed.

Any pride in their seamanship that the crew might have felt was short-lived, however, for hardly had the twin 'fish' leapt from the bows of the small boat than a great shadow fell across her; it was that of another destroyer, this time the *Herman Schömann*. Dick Saunders just had time to see that he, like his colleagues, had missed the target before flinging the helm over and streaking for home, while the water around erupted in great fountains from the destroyer's fire.

Meanwhile the first three were still intent on making good their escape, and the final hope of Hilary Gamble's boat had proved negative, when he sent his last torpedo at the destroyer; once again it failed to get away due to a faulty impulse.

It seemed that the small craft were to anticipate the fate of the six Swordfish aircraft even then making for the Nazi squadron. But then the unexpected happened, for the poor performance of one of Pumphrey's three motors (which had made his mind up to steer alongside the protective screen and not try to pierce it) suddenly righted itself as if to bestow extra impetus on the flight of *221*, although, as he said in his report, his first intention was "to attempt to fight through".

The fiasco with regard to the naval torpedo aircraft and their meagre escort was not the only one of its type that day, for the same situation was being played out again. To do their hazardous work properly, the MTBs should have protection by aircraft and also by motor gun-boats, and there were none. Indeed, the feelings of the navy towards the RAF were not ones of unalloyed benevolence; more than once the remark had been passed that the only fighters the crews had managed to spot were those of the Luftwaffe. But the observer on the spot does not always see every detail of a situation, and in fact at about this time a group of Hurricanes and the Spitfires of No 3 Squadron were in the vicinity.

It was then that events took another unexpected turn. Above the din of battle it was impossible to identify individual sounds, so that the appearance of a pair of the long-awaited MGBs was that much more dramatic.

These vessels were also based on Dover, but they were late, and their commanders, Lieutenant P. F. S. Gould DSC in No *43* and Lieutenant R. King with *41*, were not sparing the engines of the 60-foot boats now. Indeed they were racing towards the MTBs with their bows well up and sending out a long wake behind at more than 40 knots.

It was Stewart Gould in the first boat who summed up the situation: there was the *Friedrich Ihn* in full pursuit of the MTBs at such a distance that only the choppy conditions made aim difficult for her gunners. Without hesitation the two smaller vessels dashed in between the hunter and its quarry, with the gunners shooting with everything they had. This was little enough for, unlike the MTBs they resembled, these craft had no torpedoes or depth-charges but instead carried a pair of machine-guns and a 20-millimetre Oerlikon. In the narrow gap into which they had dashed, a reduction in speed was called for, but the demands of the moment could allow this to be by only a mere 5 knots, and at this speed they fought a gun duel with the destroyer and with a formation of Nazi fighters that appeared overhead. So intense was the smaller vessels' attack that after a short time the destroyer broke off the engagement where it was trapped in the crossfire of the MGBs, so that the MTBs had sufficient breathing-space to make good their escape, although Dick Saunders, the last of the group, deliberately lagged back to render what assistance he could to the air-crews he knew must inevitably need taking from the water as the pace of the engagement quickened.

Meanwhile there were other torpedo-boats racing to the scene, for Ramsgate had despatched a small flotilla a little later than those from Dover had left. They had further to travel so that their arrival on the scene coincided with a further deterioration in the weather, the haze having increased and the cloud base being lower now as the wind rose in strength. Although it was 12.25 p.m. when they left harbour, there was every hope of the three boats making contact with the Nazi squadron further to the east than the position where their colleagues had attacked, but as luck would have it, all three were troubled with engine-malfunction *en route*.

The leader of the Ramsgate boats was Lieutenant D. J. Long, in No *32* the only regular officer among the commanders. This was followed by No *18* with Sub-Lieutenant I. C. Trelawney and No *71* with another Sub-Lieutenant of the Volunteer Reserve, O. B. Mabee.

First sight of the enemy was established when a group of E-boats was spotted flanked by destroyers, and it was assumed that these were protecting the position on the larger ships' port bow and that the capital vessels would shortly be passing. In consequence the trio swung round to be in the best position for the discharge of their torpedoes. After a short wait when it was deemed undesirable to attempt to penetrate the screen and reveal their presence (the odds against them were something like one to ten among the smaller craft alone), it became clear that in fact the battle-cruisers and the cruiser had already passed so that the main targets were now in all probability some miles ahead. Obviously nothing could be accomplished now, particularly in view of the unresponsive engines, and so the flotilla withdrew without actually making contact with the enemy.

The Swordfish were now in the air, and the instrument-panel clocks were the centre of attention for the eighteen members of the crews as they circled in wait for their escort. It was as cold as only the Channel can be in winter, and visibility was at times no more than half a mile, while Manston was completely hidden from view as the six machines orbited a little to seaward.

Two minutes later a great wave of relief flooded over the men, for suddenly through the murk and below the upper layer of cloud came the welcome shapes of ten Spitfires from No 72 Squadron with Brian Kingcome in the lead, hot from Gravesend where the Squadron-Leader had mustered every pilot he could at such short notice. The fighters took up position over the biplanes, and the vigil was continued, although every moment meant that the advantage was slipping away as the enemy steamed out of range. The delay was brief. Quite suddenly Esmonde made up his mind and flung an arm above his head to muster the flight, then throttles were eased open and control columns pressed forward as the torpedo-bombers lost height to only 50 feet above the unfriendly green water as they set course for the target area fifteen minutes' flying-time away. There would be no further escort.

Meanwhile, the ten Spitfires took up position above and immediately encountered problems. With their superior speed they could outstrip their charges with ease, encumbered as the naval aircraft were with their torpedoes. The fighters therefore commenced to weave a complex pattern above, with their throttles scarcely open in an effort to stay in position; at least that way they could still keep the six Swordfish in sight, the first three in line astern spaced at about 150-foot intervals, the second group in arrow-head formation; even this was going to be difficult enough, for now it was beginning to rain.

Half way and a group of fighter shapes sprang out of the gloom. For a brief second all must have wondered if this was the remainder of the escort, but they were quickly disillusioned by the bark of machine-gun fire—not the muted chatter of weapons simulated by the film business but the sharp staccato sound of the real thing; the very thought of it, smashing into a human body, ripping living flesh from sinew, and squirming sinew from bone, induces a feeling of nausea.

There were two *Kettes** of Messerschmitt 109s, and they blasted the naval machines now, surprising their pilots as the fire passed through the fabric, mostly without inflicting damage. It required only a few seconds for the Spitfire pilots above to realize the danger to their charges, and almost as one they came screaming down onto the Nazis and began to hound them in the direction of Ramsgate. Seemingly the first fighters were no more than bait, for scarcely had the *mêlée* vanished than more Messerschmitts appeared and began to harry the biplanes. With their lack of speed, they were already a difficult target, but now the six began to jink and weave; it saved their lives, and they were still leading the fighters a grim dance when Squadron-Leader Kingcome returned with his formation so that the enemy retreated to re-form. This they did quickly, and the next moment some twenty of them came in with guns blazing to be met by three Spitfires. Only a few got through but they so set about the two lead Swordfish that they sought refuge at zero feet. Oh for a larger escort!

In fact there was one, but they had become airborne only nine minutes before the machines under Esmonde had left the rendezvous. In order to conserve time, they had headed out to sea in the hope of meeting the biplanes on the way, but when it became clear that this was impossible, precious time was lost when the Spitfires of 124 Squadron from Biggin Hill (with those from 401 Squadron at the same base) returned to Manston in search of the naval formation.

With time lost in fighting off the Messerschmitts, it was almost an hour after midday when the Swordfish arrived in sight of the Nazi fleet. The picture was a daunting one. With the three capital ships steaming in line astern, the formation of vessels was flanked by protective screens of warships including destroyers which seemed to stretch away and melt into the mist, and over all hung the smoke of battle, for already the fleet had suffered an attack by torpedo-boats which were, even then, withdrawing.

But if the position below was intimidating, above it was worse, for a veritable 'umbrella' of fighters seemed to blacken the sky from less than 100 feet altitude to 2,000 feet, and between these limits the aircraft were stacked in layers at 500-

*Kette: A group of three aircraft.

foot intervals, Messerschmitt 109s and the newer Focke-Wulf 190s. To hesitate would have been fatal, and the ten Spitfires dropped their noses and dived into phalanx—and immediately became as lost as small pebbles dropped into dry sand.

Then the guns opened up. At first the fire was careful, for there were many Nazi fighters in the area, and over the outer screen the slow biplanes flying low down with their fabric all shot away and streaming back in ragged ribbons from the earlier engagement presented no immediate danger. Unknown to their pilots, the missing Spitfires from Biggin Hill now appeared on the scene after a wild dash out over the sea from Manston, but they were swiftly swallowed up by the sky full of fighting aeroplanes.

Over the outer screen of Nazi torpedo-boats, and with the most concentrated barrage of fire behind them, the six biplanes now had a new hazard: the destroyers and cruisers beyond were firing their heavier guns so that the shells threw up huge columns of water in the form of a great wall, any part of which could smack the frail aircraft out of the sky like swatting an insect.

Despite this daunting curtain which the 11-inch guns were making, Esmonde led his little band on, over the inner screen and straight at the leading *Scharnhorst*.

Meanwhile more Spitfires arrived, this time from the Hornchurch Wing, in a vain attempt to find the Swordfish still at the rendezvous point. Unlike the earlier ones, which had been searching over-far to the south, these were too late. Trusting that the Calais area might reveal something, they made off to that part of the French coast, completely oblivious of the pocket of hell that was hidden in the mist. They found nothing and after a brief patrol returned to base.

Fifty yards behind the first torpedo-bomber came the one piloted by Sub-Lieutenant Brian Rose, carrying Sub-Lieutenant Edgar Lee as his observer, while Colin Kingsmill, with observer R. M. Samples, also a Sub-Lieutenant, and Leading Airman D. A. Bunce as gunner, brought up the rear of the first section. It was then that the pilots of the protecting Spitfires overhead were treated to a fleeing spectacle of an astonishing nature when they could relax concentration from fighting for their own lives.

Almost over the inner screen, Eugene Esmonde's aircraft was now the centre of attention, not only for the anti-aircraft fire from below (which had cut great gaping holes in its sides with tatters of fabric streaming back from them) but, minutes later, for swarms of Messerschmitt 109s that formed up to pump a deadly fire into the seemingly indestructible target in a desperate attempt to destroy it before it could launch its deadly torpedo at the battle-cruiser.

Pilots above glanced down and momentarily thought they saw a man out of the cockpit. They glanced again, and it was confirmed, for there, sitting astride the rear of the battered fuselage, unprotected from the icy blast of the slipstream and seemingly oblivious of the whirling holocaust going on around, sat the formation-leader's gunner, Leading Airman W. J. Clinton, gripping with his legs like a horseman while he beat out the flaming fabric with his thickly gloved hands.

Although the emphasis of the fighter attacks were now concentrated on the second section of three Swordfish, Brian Rose's machine was not escaping in the first flight. At almost the same moment as the gunner ahead was performing his astounding act of bravery, the fire from below faded once more. This could mean only one thing—fighters, and in a trice there they were, not Messerschmitts this time but menacing blunt-nosed Focke-Wulf 190s with gaily coloured spinners and little twinkling lights in the front of the wings. Those lights meant death. Their pilots were firing as they came round in a great sweeping arc and presenting a strange sight as they did so with flaps and undercarriage down to slow them sufficiently to bring their guns to bear on the slow, staggering biplanes. Ahead, Clinton was back in the cockpit and crouched over his gun in an effort to support Leading Airman Johnson, his compatriot, in Rose's machine, who was trying to beat off the Focke-Wulfs with his rifle calibre Lewis. Then, quite suddenly, the rattle of this gun ceased. Aware that something had happened, Edgar Lee turned to see Johnson slumped forward and obviously stone dead. He reached back and attempted to lift the corpse from over the rear of the gun that now poked uselessly skywards: it was impossible. With the resource that has always marked naval men, he did the next best thing and stood up to get a better view of his attackers, yelling to the pilot when each was approaching so that they might swerve towards each one, causing it to overshoot or break away to avoid a collision.

With his observer bellowing away behind, Rose had to concentrate his attention ahead as the fleet, making a good 30 knots, still loomed larger beyond 'Winkle' Esmonde's lead. He was actually fixing his gaze on this when the lower port wing vanished as if ripped off by the hand of a malevolent giant, struck off by an 11-inch shell fired to contribute to the carpet barrage but ricocheting off the water. Yet still the machine kept on.

They were beyond the second screen now, a fact that they noted with surprise, but for Brian Rose concentration was reaching impossibility. In the first of the attacks by the Focke-Wulfs he had been wounded himself by wicket splinters of steel from an exploding shell driven into his back. In a moment, the Swordfish had toppled over and dipped dangerously near to the surface of the water, and it was only the bellowed orders from his observer that had forced him to hold off the blackness that threatened to engulf him, groan an acknowledgement and haul on the control column so that the sweat poured into his eyes from the exertion.

Seemingly taking note that the first of the menacing birds was winged, the Focke-Wulfs swarmed again about the damaged lead machine, still with their landing-gear dangling so that they looked like birds of prey about to strike, as one witness recalls them. The first burst of fire killed Lieutenant W. H. Williams, the observer, and W. J. Clinton who had so recently attempted to save the Swordfish from a fiery end. At the same time the fire tore open Esmonde's back and severely wounded him in the head; yet still, the crazy, mutilated machine flew on.

By all medical standards the pilot should now have been dead, but by some unaccountable effort of will Eugene Esmonde hung on to a semblance of conscious life, although the blood from his head-wounds was now flowing freely over the discoloured fleece lining of his leather flying-jacket that was all torn away behind and exposing the tortured flesh. He brought the nose of his machine up slightly as the bulk of the *Scharnhorst* filled his vision at less than 1,500 yards' range, and released his torpedo.

Unknowing that the deadly 'fish' no longer hung between the

spread legs of the failing biplane, the fighters came on again, about fifteen of them in an untidy gaggle of Messerschmitts and Focke-Wulfs. By now Esmonde had certainly joined his crew in death but in doing so must have locked the controls with a grip that for the moment kept the machine going in a long, steady descent so that it seemed to be on a target-run. A burst of cannon-fire from one of the Focke-Wulf 190s carried away the upper centre-section of the doomed biplane, and with that it dropped into the sea and immediately sank, taking with it the bodies of the three brave occupants to a sailors' tomb in sight of Ramsgate. Meanwhile, the torpedo which seemed to be running true went wide as the steersman of the big Nazi battle-cruiser spun the wheel in violent evasive action.

The twisting course that the second machine of the lead section had been forced to steer to avoid the fore and aft attentions of the fighters meant that there was a short delay before the next torpedo was delivered, for not only were Rose's wounds beginning to stiffen but he now found that his left arm was almost useless, probably hurt when the shell exploding against the aircraft structure had driven splinters into his back. Then, quite suddenly it seemed, the *Gneisenau* loomed massively ahead. At that moment a blow seemed to lift the nose of the aircraft from underneath, and the engine began to falter. What had happened was that the fuel-tank had been holed and the petrol was flooding back over the fuselage. At this, Lee stopped screaming the directions of 'Port' and 'Starboard' to his pilot and instead yelled to him to keep the nose up and switch to the emergency tank. Then, as the motor responded to the fresh injection of life-giving spirit, a battle-cruiser lay dead ahead, and Rose's failing senses were rallied for the last time as a seemingly distant voice bid him drop his torpedo. The range was 1,200 yards.

Free of its load, the Swordfish seemed to gain fresh energy, and it answered to the controls more readily as the pilot hauled it at zero feet over the decks of the wildly swinging ship. Underneath them the faces of the brave sailors upturned as so many white blobs as the biplane avoided a collision with the superstructure: then they saw that it was at the *Prinz Eugen* that they had aimed, and the skill of the man at the wheel had ensured that they too had missed.

As the elderly biplane seemed to claw its painful way upwards, the fire from below faded away, and chivalrously the German fighter pilots drew off. The British machine could no longer harm their charges, and they turned their attention to the final machine of Section One.

This was flown by Colin Kingsmill, and as it came in over the destroyer screen, it took so much damage from the anti-aircraft gunners that it is surprising it was still flyable when it emerged. Clear of this, it came in for attention from the fighters. They did their work well, and one of the first passes by a Focke-Wulf sent a burst of fire into the Pegasus motor which sheered away the two upper cylinders.

However, the Nazi machines were not having it all their own way, and in the rear seat Leading Airman D. A. Bunce was working with the Lewis gun like one possessed. Two would-be executioners hung on to the tail of the Swordfish at each side and countered every turn with a burst of fire from that direction. Over-confident, they stayed too long, and Bunce was able to put a deadly stream of bullets into one so that it heeled over and went into the sea that was being sent into an eruption of water from the falling missiles exchanged between the vessels locked in combat below. Then the remains of the engine took fire, and in a few seconds the flames licked back to set light to one wing of the Swordfish.

Like his crew behind, Kingsmill had been wounded earlier, but the difficulty of controlling such a heavily punished aircraft was making impossible demands on his failing strength. At 2,000 yards distance from the *Prinz Eugen*, the torpedo was released, and the machine, now blazing like a torch in the weak February light, turned away as the pilot searched for somewhere to ditch.

It was not long before a suitable cluster of vessels appeared at the after end of the vast convoy. As the Swordfish hove in sight, it was greeted by a hail of fire, and the crew realized their mistake, having chosen to put down among a group of E-boats. Staggering away, the Sub-Lieutenant sought sanctuary elsewhere, but his choice ran out when the motor stopped, and at the low altitude they were left no alternative than to drop into the water.

In fact the spot could scarcely have been better picked for it was not far from some British MTBs, and the look-out on one quickly spotted the situation so that before long the vessel was closing the few hundred yards that separated it from the three severely wounded men who were now struggling in the water; their inflatable dinghy had been destroyed in the fire, since it was carried stowed in the upper main-plane.

Meanwhile, Sub-Lieutenant Brian Rose was coaxing his riddled Swordfish to a respectable altitude, at the same time making what progress he could towards the comparative safety of the port wing of the destroyer screen. He reached 1,200 feet and gave the question of his future action brief thought: with the reserve fuel tank (on which they had been flying since the puncture of the main one) now seriously depleted, there was no hope of limping back to base, and the pain in his arm was increasing. He turned the stricken biplane in the general direction of the battle's fringe and put what space he could between himself and the centre of the holocaust, with the idea of putting down on the sea.

Having flown only a short distance, the release from the immediate demands of penetrating the battle-cruisers' protective screens allowed consciousness of his mutilated arm to take over, and soon the pain was such that it swamped everything; even his vision was intermittently impaired by the waves of agony that threatened to engulf him, so that controlling the wallowing machine was more by unconscious training. Ahead, he thought he saw a group of British MTBs and wondered if they would be a haven beside which to come down; then, still some 4 miles away, his mind was made up for him when the tortured Pegasus motor faltered and finally stopped. He glided the remaining distance and pulled back on the control column. With a final lurch that drew an involuntary gasp of agony from the wounded Rose, "the Swordfish sat down very nicely," as he was later to put it.

Once in the comparative safety of the water, the two had now to capture the bright yellow dinghy which leapt and hissed at the end of a line nearby as it automatically inflated. Edgar Lee did his best to prize the body of gunner Johnson out of the rear cockpit, but, with the observer's weakness after the ordeal of the fight and the awkward way that the dead man was wedged in, it proved as impossible to do this now as it had been in flight.

Rose was in no position to assist since his left arm hung useless and mercifully now devoid of feeling in the cold. However, with his one good arm he was able to right the inflated dinghy which was bobbing a short distance off, and into this he more or less tumbled while his observer tried to steady it as the little craft rose and fell on the moving water. Edgar Lee then turned again for a final effort to drag the corpse out, but at the moment the hulk of the Swordfish began to roll over before going under. He thereupon toppled into the dinghy and pulled at the restraining line, fearful that they would be dragged down with the aircraft. The knot refused to budge, and he managed to untangle it only moments before the aircraft broke like a jack-knife and vanished into the depths.

The MTBs amongst which they had ditched seemed reluctant to make any rescue-attempt as far as the two could see in the worsening visibility—small wonder in view of the fact that the British vessels were locked in an engagement of their own with Nazi E-boats. So the young flying officers began a three-handed paddle in what appeared to be the right direction, although each rising wave flung them up between the exchange of fire. Progress was hideously slow since every few yards they had to stop to bale out the accumulated water, to the accompaniment of groans from Rose whose arm was now regaining feeling by the physical effort of the last few minutes.

It was while the pair were lying prone in the bottom of the boat that they thought of using some of the distress-flares to mark their position, and in the bag with these they discovered a tin of aluminium powder which would stain the sea with a bright metallic pool about them. Lee broke the tin open and flung the powder into the waves, but he was so overwrought that he failed to take note of the wind, which tossed the dust back over the two, so that, when next they had to crouch to try to escape the murderous cross-fire that was still being exchanged, they looked like nothing so much as a pair of bright metal robots. However, when next they resumed the baling, the parts of the tin served better than their flying-helmets had done previously. The baling went on for some two hours, interspersed with firing of flares. With one of these, Lee came close to killing his companion, for it was only at the last moment that he realized he was pointing it at the other's face instead of skywards.

By now, the worst of the sea engagement had passed their position 11 miles off South Foreland, and an MTB with Anti-Submarine Boat *31* was sweeping the area for survivors, the *31* having already picked up Kingsmill and the others from their Swordfish 8 miles off North Foreland at 2.15 p.m. One of these vessels suddenly increased speed, making for the rush of red flame that the look-out had spotted. As the two hove in sight of the dinghy, the men on deck hailed the figures in the little yellow craft, but their shouts were indistinct and went un-heeded as Rose and Lee maintained silence believing that the vessels were in fact E-boats. They were therefore surprised when able to distinguish that they were being hailed in English.

As the MTB and MASB came alongside, the nearest with a bold '44' on its bow, eager hands were held out to drag Lee aboard. Numb as he was, his position was not so bad as that of his pilot, who was almost helpless. Without hesitation one of the sailors from the boat leapt into the freezing water and helped Brian Rose on board. The light was fast beginning to fade as another of the torpedo-boat's crew glanced at his watch and addressed an unanswered question to nobody in particular. "Are there any others out there?" It was just 2.45 p.m.

If the speaker meant crews of Swordfish aircraft, he might have been satisfied more than two hours before, since the three machines of Eugene Esmonde's second section had still to drop their torpedoes. The leader of this group was Lieutenant J. C. Thompson, flying with Sub-Lieutenant Parkinson as observer while Leading Airman E. Topping manned the gun aft, in the machine spearheading the 'vic' formation. On his starboard side flew Sub-Lieutenant C. R. Wood with Fuller-Wright, while Leading Airman Wheeler was in charge of the Lewis gun that was their sole rear defence. On the other side were two more Sub-Lieutenants, Peter Bligh and Bill Beynon, while Leading Airman Smith crouched over the gun and surveyed the sky in the region from which attack was most likely to come.

It was not long in doing so. Before the three aircraft had reached the outer screen three Focke-Wulfs, their pilots having selected flaps and undercarriage down to reduce speed to ap proximate with that of the sluggish biplanes, were hanging on the formation and blasting its members whenever they could. At all costs the three ships must be saved, and any one of the staggering biplanes could mean the end.

By now the order 'Open Visor' had been passed to the Luft-waffe fighter pilots, a code-word which cancelled the strict radio silence that had been observed up to now. Interceptions were being directed by fighter-controllers on the ships in the convoy itself. As a further part of the general defence strategy, the heavy fire from the ships' 6-inch guns was of comparatively low trajectory, lethal for low-flying torpedo aircraft but at the same time allowing the defending fighter plenty of scope. By and large these had operated at less than 1,000 feet during the radio silence so that attacking machines could be picked out im-mediately in the zone of clear air above the vessels and there immediately engaged either by fighters or by the light anti-aircraft fire from the ships, which included that from machine-gun nests high on the masts of some destroyers.

The Messerschmitt 109s and Focke-Wulf 190s were at this point operating only just beyond the proximity of their own bases in northern France but could now do so at a variety of altitudes, as the situation demanded. However, this was of little consequence to the crews of the final section of Swordfish which were losing height as they approached the second screen. They had not weathered the encounter with the Focke-Wulfs without hurt, for as they continued to hold disciplined formation and drop lower still, they presented a picture as of three flying rag-bags with large sections of their fabric covering shot away and great streamers of that which remained flapping in the slipstream. The steel tube and duralumin structure with linen covering had, however, proved in the past to be capable of absorbing a tremendous amount of battle-damage without dis-integrating, and the state of this trio was re-endorsing the fact.

The same can hardly be said for the human body, and as the 'vic' weathered the second screen without apparent further punishment, it seems unlikely that some of the crews were not already dead or mortally wounded.

A third and final barrier was the water barrage that was still being thrown up by the concentrated fire from the 11-inch guns. At this moment, by some freak of circumstance, a lull took place in the fighting. Even the harrying fighters drew off, perhaps because it was now necessary to spread the cover to higher levels since avoidance of British radar was now futile. In comparative silence, broken only by a macabre background music from the exchange of light fire between the vessels below, the seemingly indestructible little band flew beyond the curtain of water like unruffled actors taking a final bow.

What became of them beyond will never be known. They simply flew into oblivion and were never seen again, taking violent evasive action and about to commence their run to the target as they did so. It is officially assumed that they were able to loose their torpedoes, but there were no survivors to tell of their colleagues' fate, although two bodies were later recovered from the sea. The time was about one o'clock, scarcely more than forty minutes since the six doomed naval machines had bumped across the snow-patched grass at Manston beside the road to Margate.

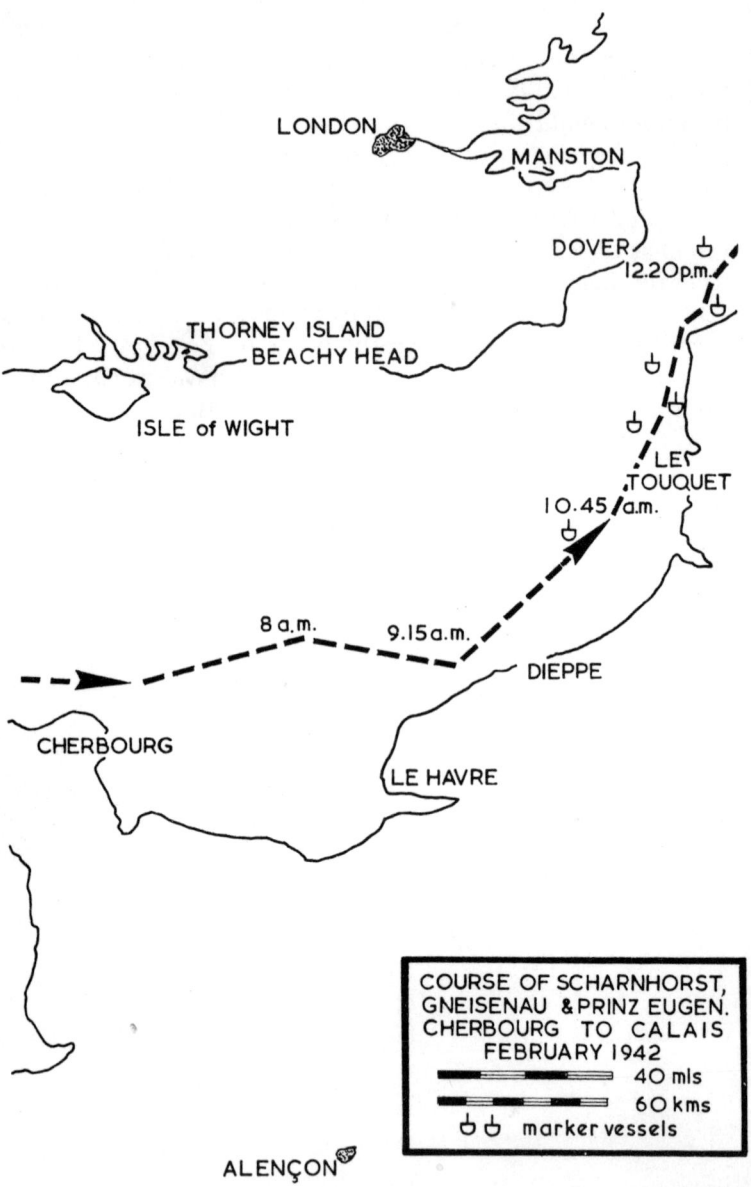

The course of the Nazi warships between Cherbourg and Calais

7

No Quarter

The six torpedo-bombers from Manston had undertaken their intended mission on the final decision alone of Eugene Esmonde. He was never at any time under orders to carry out the sortie, but he knew what was expected of him and his fellows, to attack and if possible sink the Nazi battle-cruisers and the single cruiser. That and that alone was the reason why the little detachment was in Kent while the remainder of 825 Squadron, after its re-formation at Lee-on-Solent, had gone to Arbroath.

Sensible of the history that was being made that day, Vice-Admiral B. H. Ramsay had written only a short time later: "In my opinion the gallant sortie of these six Swordfish constitutes one of the finest exhibitions of self-sacrifice and devotion to duty that the war has yet witnessed." In similar vein Wing-Commander Gleave (who knew all about personal suffering since the day less than two years before when he had been forced to leave his blazing Hurricane "in great haste" not far from Biggin Hill) had retired soberly to his office and concluded a report to Air Vice-Marshal Leigh-Mallory with words that are probably unique, for Esmonde was a Royal Navy Officer not in his command: "I am of the opinion that Lieutenant-Commander Esmonde is well worthy of the posthumous award of the Victoria Cross." Scarcely more than a month later the suggestion was acted upon, and in the *London Gazette*'s announcement of the fact it was also added that all the surviving officers were to receive the DSO from His Majesty King George VI, while gunner Donald Bunce was to be awarded the Conspicuous Gallantry Medal.

But 'gongs' can only reward the living or make a gesture to the memory of the dead; they cannot alleviate human suffering.

As Tom Gleave sat at his desk to write the report, in the outer office a WAAF tried to see her paper-work through red-rimmed, tear-dimmed eyes. Her boy-friend had worn a darker blue and that lunchtime had died with Esmonde's squadron in the icy waters of the cruel sea.

In a personal rage at the waste of lives in this manner, Admiral Ramsay again put pen to paper and sent a signal to the Fleet Air Arm at Lee-on-Solent, while, at the risk of a court-martial, the senior radar officer from Swingate took courage from the Admiral and wrote an outspoken criticism of the action. In fact, this was to come into the hands of Winston Churchill, and although he passed it to Leigh-Mallory there were no repercussions, despite the fact that the Air Vice-Marshal swung the blame onto Coastal Command's AOC-in-C. Churchill was more interested in winning the war than in finding scapegoats. Henceforth a large part of the action was to take place in the grey skies of the Channel anyway.

What may be the first of these major aerial sorties occurred at exactly twenty-seven minutes past eleven, with the take-off of the vanguard of 243 bombers that were to continue the assault until the gathering dusk of the winter's evening put an end to matters seven hours later. But it would be unfair to give the impression that the Royal Navy had shot its final bolt, for already six elderly destroyers, all in excess of two decades old had slipped out of Harwich with Captain Pizey leading in the flagship *Campbell*. The remainder of Flotillas 21 and 16 was made up of *Mackay*, *Vivacious*, *Walpole*, *Whitshed* and *Worcester*.

The problems associated with bombing the ships were many, but they were common to all the Groups involved, ranging from No 2 with its light machines to No 5, perhaps the most powerful in the Command, which included Avro Manchester squadrons as well as two flying the better type derived from it, the Lancaster, although the latter were officially not yet operational.

These dilemmas were all brought about by the prevailing weather, which in places restricted visibility to as little as 2,000 yards, although it was frequently less, the cloud-base half an hour later being recorded as below 1,000 feet. From this it is quite plain that armour-piercing bombs were ruled out, for these would require to be dropped from sufficient height to pass through the thick decks of the large vessels, and this in turn called for sufficient visibility to aim correctly. In consequence other general-purpose bombs had to be substituted. Although with luck they might damage a vessel enough for it to be forced to reduce speed to a point where it could be finished off with torpedoes, all too often they merely bounced off the armoured decks and exploded harmlessly in the water.

A second problem was that of finding the Nazi squadron at all, and in fact almost two hundred bombers failed to find the target, only thirty-nine actually doing so and carrying out an attack. Some fifteen were lost, but of this number how many were accounted for by anti-aircraft fire or fighters will probably never be known, for it is certain that some would just have flown into the sea (as did those of Coastal Command, often while engaged in mine-laying, the pilots unable to distinguish between it and the sky under the weather conditions). Nevertheless it would be wrong to lay blame over-much on the weather. That is what was done in some circles at the time to hide a combination of stupidity, inefficiency and lack of communication.

The five squadrons of Spitfires, all Mark Vbs, which were supposed to protect the Swordfish, had taken off between 12.18 p.m. and 12.25 p.m., and those which failed to make their rendezvous had patrolled the Straits. It is interesting at this point to note such was the confusion over the Channel that members of No 72 Squadron reported observing strikes "attributed to torpedoes". Subsequent Intelligence reports suggested that the air fighting had accounted for three enemy aircraft in addition to two probables and nine damaged, for the loss of a single Spitfire and its pilot.

In an operation of this nature the destruction of the capital vessels is the main objective, but to do this it is also necessary to strike at the escort shipping, and so Hurricane fighters were forced into use. These were of the Mark IIB variety, then a relatively new introduction which, in addition to provision for two 250- or 500-pound bombs under the wings, had also an armament of twelve Browning machine-guns. The first group of these fighters, ten in number, was despatched at twenty minutes to one, and their objective was the escort vessels. The punishment that could be inflicted by an attack from machines like this from low altitude is very great indeed, for even on a large vessel the best-protected position on a deck is still relatively exposed. This is even more true of smaller boats. It is symptomatic of the day that the pilots failed to find the flotilla and instead lost one of their number in strafing a group of minesweepers off Boulogne.

Over the part of the Channel where the *Scharnhorst, Gneisenau* and *Prinz Eugen* were now making good speed again, it had just begun to rain once more. Great wreaths of mist curled up into the cloud, so that at times the perspex hoods of the fighters appeared to be obliterated by the elements. With the cold rain lancing down there arrived the Canadian fighters. At last, after the abortive attempt to find the Swordfish, they were over the battle area in the shape of 401 Squadron with the Spitfires of No 124. Almost immediately they were in the thick of the fighting, and a formation of Messerschmitt 109s swooped on them with guns blazing. Sergeant Morrison and Pilot Officer Harley each took a quick burst at a 109, but such was the whirling confusion of the fight that they had to leave the killing undone and turn away to prevent others setting on their tails. The first Messerschmitt struggled on severely winged, like a wounded bird. A moment later a third Spitfire was careering down on the stricken Nazi with guns blazing. For a moment the splinter-camouflaged fighter with the pale blue sides (now contrasting strongly with the leaden hue of the sky that formed a backdrop) seemed to hang in the air; then the machine reared up before dropping on a wing to plunge down to the icy waters beneath, leaving a great streak of greasy black smoke hanging in the air to mark its grave.

At almost the same moment another of the same type crossed incautiously close to the fighter with Canadian Pilot Officer Ormston at the controls. It was a moment's work to squeeze the gun-button at the top of the grip on his control column. The cockpit was suddenly filled with the stench of cordite fumes, and in a trice the Messerschmitt was plummeting earthwards with parts breaking off as it went down. For a moment it looked as if the sea was to be its resting-place, as it had been for its fellow, but then it flattened out just long enough to change its trajectory. As the men at the guns sensed the danger and scattered like the sudden opening of a flower, the 109 came full bore on to the deck of a destroyer with a thunderclap like the slamming of the gates of Hell itself, and the great burst of flame from the explosion momentarily lit up the surrounding gloom like a dozen suns.

Meanwhile, in another part of the same patch of sky there were other British fighters, blasting away for their lives like the others in the *mêlée* with their four nose-mounted cannon. These strange-looking machines with high, prominent tailplanes were Westland Whirlwinds, twin-engined single-seaters. In fact, due to the extreme secrecy then in force (which was even now sending pilots and naval crews to intercept ships of undisclosed type), the Whirlwind was supposed to be still on the Secret List, and the publication of its details was forbidden in Britain, despite the existence of Nazi training-manuals giving full details and including British official silhouettes! Now, at a little past 1 p.m., ten of them from No 137 Squadron at Matlaske were supposed to be providing top cover for destroyers which they failed to find, discovering instead the Nazi fleet inside a whole array of marker-ships and approaching Ostend. They were immediately set upon by the protective shield of Messerschmitt 109s and Focke-Wulf 190s so that only six survived to make the return journey.

Closely following them into the shifting battle-zone came a dozen Spitfires and eight Hurricanes. They were IICs this time, armed with four deadly Hispano cannon of 20-millimetre bore. Thus equipped, they were ideal to deliver a low-level attack on the destroyers forming the inner screen, and, negotiating the fire from the outer barrier of E- and R-boats, this is what they proceeded to do. With the gunners huddled behind their shields (which offered some protection over the breaches of their weapons) and pouring up a veritable curtain of fire, the single-seat fighters came down low, and lower still. Then, in a seeming rush as they came closer, they roared over, seeming scarcely to miss the superstructure. The pilots could see the faces of the crews suddenly upturned and white as they roared overhead, while the sound of their cannon shells on the surrounding decks added to the din.

It seemed impossible that they could miss, and they did not, but such are the problems of aerial warfare that no more could be claimed than that "cannon strikes were seen". This had been the third attempt that Hurricanes had made to find the enemy, the first sortie having begun at 12.40 p.m. when 607 took off from Manston. They had failed to find anything of note in the way of targets, although some fire was exchanged with what was probably returning marker-boats. This tempted the formation too close to the shore defences, and one Hurricane fell to the guns there.

The second attempt, at 1.18 p.m., was no more successful, although they penetrated as far as Gravelines, and the final sortie flown from Tangmere was the first actually to engage the enemy, although at a cost of four machines from which only one pilot was rescued. No 607 Squadron's Hurricanes were back in the fight with an escort of Spitfires, but, 'bounced' by a Messerschmitt patrol, they lost their protective cover and had to be content with shooting up a couple of supply-ships for which they paid dearly with a loss of three machines. Such was the confusion that only present-day research has established the truth of even this small facet of the battle, for contemporary Intelligence reports confused this action with one against nine destroyers.

Spectacular as these operations were, they could do no more than harry the smaller Nazi vessels and were incapable of striking at the primary targets. The only way to do this was by means of torpedo-bombers and thus it was that No 217's Bristol Beauforts moved to the centre of the stage. Based at St Eval, they had been ordered to Thorney Island. They were only seven in number, a difficult-sized group since, ideally, the official instructions laid down, an attack of this nature against a well-escorted and fast-moving flotilla of naval vessels in daylight should be delivered by "at least . . . twelve aircraft for each target".

At almost midday arrangements were made with 11 Group for a fighter escort to be provided, but this could not positively be agreed as the fighters were required to escort the Swordfish. However, every effort was promised to meet the needs of the seven Beauforts that were to rendezvous Manston in half an hour. No one could foresee that the tryst could never be kept due to a multitude of errors,,a combination of circumstances that was to deny the Beauforts being over the target at the same time as the naval torpedo-bombers so that the doomed six had to go it alone with no hope of a concerted attack.

At Thorney all was activity, and the loads were taken to the aircraft. Unfortunately two of the planes were not fitted with torpedoes so that a delay occurred while this was corrected, and during that period a third machine developed a mechanical fault that proved difficult to trace, thus holding up the departure of the complete group.

It was only five minutes before the time scheduled to meet the three squadrons of Kenley Spitfires over Manston that the four properly armed and serviceable machines took off, their pilots knowing full well that it was impossible to complete the journey in time, since some 120 miles separated them. Although they undertook to make the trip with all speed, it must be admitted that it was only the call of discipline which urged them on, for so close was the cloak of security drawn that they had no idea what it was they were supposed to be attacking.

Twenty minutes or so later the four were at the Kent rendez-vous, but by this time the fighters had gone and were under orders to take up escort over the battle-zone. Thus an extra quarter of an hour was flung away until two of the pilots on their own initiative decided to break away and make for the target alone, and it was an additional misfortune that the remaining pair observed nothing of this in the confusion of circling machines over Manston so they joined the rear of a group of Hudson aircraft and eventually landed as the fuel position was becoming critical. The crews were here re-briefed and set off into the rain that was now beginning to fall in a steady down-pour. Meanwhile the three stragglers had got away from Thorney and arrived at Manston. They were given the latest position of the target by radio before setting off in the wake of the earlier machines of No 217 Squadron. There could be no concerted attack now, only individual ones, and already more than an hour had been lost; the first of them would not arrive until twenty minutes to four in the afternoon. Meanwhile the fighters, which again included No 3 Squadron, were swallowed up in the *mêlée*.

While this charade was being played out at home, the crews of the three warships were, with their satellites, fighting against one enemy or another, so that it was almost a relief when a look-out pointed out an object drifting near to the *Scharnhorst*. Glasses were focused, and sure enough there, only 100 metres off the port quarter, bobbed a drifting mine which could easily have marked the end of them all.

At about the same time the log of the leading battle-cruiser was occupied mainly with recording fights involving Messer-schmitts and British Whirlwinds, five of which are stated to have been attacking the *Gneisenau* although they could hope to do no more than make a nuisance of themselves, while a few minutes later the gunners on the *Prinz Eugen* claimed to have accounted for one of a pair of four-engined bombers, perhaps Short Stir-lings.

In the rain, wind and low cloud it was no longer possible for the three major ships to see each other, but the sound that now echoed over the squadron was one known to all seasoned mariners of the day and was among the most-feared: the rum-bling boom that indicates a mine exploding under water. In an instant part of the orderly *Scharnhorst* was tossed into confusion as water came pouring in, while at the same moment equipment was flung about the heads of the men between decks, who were plunged into darkness as the generators stopped; the direction-finder and the echo-sounder were paralysed. *Scharnhorst* im-mediately lost speed and was swung away from the line of ships on the safer French side of the charted course, but it was clear that she would have to heave to and risk the possibility of being found by British reconnaissance aircraft.

With electrical power gone, the control room on the flagship had no means of communication with the fighters or anyone else, so at this point Admiral Ciliax decided to transfer his command by taking himself and his staff aboard the destroyer *Z-29*. The smaller ship came alongside, collided, ripped a piece out of the battle-cruiser and swung away to hit the fenders. In that moment, scarcely five minutes after the explosion, the Admiral and his officers jumped from the heaving deck onto the adjacent one and were gone. A few minutes later the *Gneisenau* and *Prinz Eugen* raced past, leaving the former flagship with a token protection of four small craft alone, with silent radios and cut off even from the sight of the others of the flotilla by the visibility, now down to only one mile. There followed the most nerve-wracking period any of the crew could remember, hove to at a negligible distance from the enemy coast while the engin-eers and damage-repair crews toiled in the claustrophobic space between decks, while all the time the look-outs kept their senses alert for any indication that they were discovered. One RAF machine looming out of the fog could spell their end—but none came. About three o'clock they were under way again, and the brave and redoubtable Captain Hoffmann was guiding his ship between the other hidden mines and treacherous sandbanks at a good 25 knots or more.

The British aircraft that had taken off about twenty minutes or so before the explosion from the *Scharnhorst* were now converging over the battle area. From Debden had come the Hurricane fighters of No 11 Squadron, together with the Spitfires of No 65. By the claimed destruction of three Nazi Luftwaffe machines the former were to earn a letter of commendation from Sir Trafford Leigh-Mallory, and it was generally agreed that at this time the tactics included an attempt to draw the attackers away from the ships and towards the coast of Belgium.

This period was one of the greatest fighter activity, with Spitfires from Nos 64, 91 and 401 now acting as escort for Wellington bombers, and 411 Squadron from Hornchurch plus the Tangmere Hurricanes from 607 all present (among others). This concentration caused the maintenance of more than twenty Me 109s and F-W 190s in the protective umbrella, so that, despite a further deterioration in the weather, fights were going on now all the time. A further attack was mounted with Whirlwinds sent in, operating in pairs, and one had scarcely appeared than it was sent into the sea. A few minutes later another went down, a victim of the vigilant protective fighters, carving a long black gash of smoke across the sky from a burning engine before it fell into the water.

Strangely enough, German seamen agreed that many of the British attacks seemed to be concentrated on the *Z-29*, but they met with no success in stopping her, and as time passed, the operation became increasingly dominated by bombers that made good use of the cover afforded by the cloud, the base of which was now down to a minimum of 500 feet. Although the capital ships, when they were found, seemed to have a charmed existence, others fared less well. The patrol-ship *V1302* was lost, and *Jaguar* and the torpedo-boat *T13*, one of the group originally detailed to protect the stranded *Scharnhorst*, both suffered damage.

Among the earliest bomber take-offs had been one from

Swanton Morley mounted by American Douglas Bostons of No
226 Squadron in conjunction with similar machines of No 88.
Ten machines were involved in what was to be the operational
début of the type, so that it is unfortunate that no less than nine
of these machines failed to find the Nazi squadron, leaving a
single aircraft to make a lone attack with negligible recorded
results. Both units had flown from bases in Norfolk, No 88
operating out of Attlebridge.

Apart from the notable four-motor exceptions (such as the
Halifax bombers flown by No 35 Squadron which was typical
and the Stirlings that had previously pounded the 'ugly sisters'
with, on occasion, armour-piercing bombs when they lay at
Brest or La Pallice), the largest number of bombers was made
up from Vickers Wellingtons, operated in groups of varying size
from the four from No 40 that departed from Alconbury to the
dozen that No 241 at Stradishall was to send into action during
the later part of the day.

By now it was mid-afternoon, and the bedevilled Bristol
Beauforts had arrived at the scene at much the same time as the
destroyers under Captain Pizey. The former at once found
themselves operating under conditions that were very far from
the idealized ones imagined by the authors of the typewritten
tactical manuals. There could be no 'waves' of attackers, and
the weather precluded any attempt to 'develop' the attack 10-15
miles from the target. One instruction that could be obeyed, however, was that the force should go in at only 50 feet above the
wave tops. But the adoption of this technique is not the end of
the matter, for in order to make sure that an aerial torpedo is
running true, it is necessary that two factors are taken into
consideration when the missile is about to enter the water. The
first of these is that its axis at the centre of gravity should
subtend a slightly nose-up angle with its trajectory, while the
second demands that this should be between twelve and twenty-
four degrees below the horizontal. Secret instructions covering
eighteen sheets comprised all aspects of the technique, but on
not one was there any mention that they had to be followed
under weather conditions often far from ideal and while a whole
host of enemies were doing their best to blast their assailant out
of the sky. This was now no surprise to the Beauforts as they
approached the position where the warships were reputed to be.

It was a case of the ships finding the second pair of aircraft rather than the other way about, for, despite flying through a frenzy of activity, the first sign that they were over enemy shipping was when a line of tracer cut between the two machines, only to be closely followed by anti-aircraft bursts. As the machines lost height as a preliminary to delivering the attack, this fire became increasingly accurate, and the approaches, first from the port side and then from ahead on the starboard quarter, were both prevented by it.

The third attempt was on the final ship's port beam. At about 2,000 yards the torpedo-release was pressed, but alas there came no answering response, no change in the pilot's 'feel' of his aircraft, for the missile remained firmly in its crutch. Desperately he pulled the machine up and went round again, now harried by a couple of Messerschmitts. This time the torpedo dropped away, but it was impossible to observe its run, for immediately a life-and-death struggle began with the fighters; it ended only when one was sent plummeting down into the sea. The first that the pilot knew of this was when a yell of jubilation came over the intercom at the same time as the staccato rattle of the rear gun ceased and the doomed Messerschmitt, with smoke pouring from the engine, sent up a fountain of water beneath. The first pair of Beauforts, searching 50 miles off course, failed to find the ships.

Both the torpedoes that were dropped failed to hit a target that afternoon, although one was so close that even official reports on the following day claim a strike on a battle-cruiser. One of the Beauforts was brought down either by fighters or by anti-aircraft fire, but the conditions under which the attack had to be carried out are best summed up by one of the Beaufort pilots who reported on his return to base, "We were so low that it was difficult to discover where sea and air began; there was low cloud, rain and sleet."

Meanwhile the remaining three Beauforts had found themselves a degree of top cover only and were within striking-distance of the Nazi squadron in the vicinity of Rotterdam. Once again it was a case of the ships giving away their position by the hail of fire that greeted the first torpedo-bomber, although simultaneously the aircraft's radar was registering a strong blip caused by the vessels below the cloud. To escape from some of the fire, the pilot made a wide circle over the Dutch coast only to be handled with similar roughness by the anti-aircraft batteries there. Breaking away, he made a long, low approach over the sea towards what he believed was the *Gneisenau*, and as the battle-cruiser loomed large in his vision, the torpedo-release was pulled. As had happened with his colleague earlier, there came no response, indicating that the 'fish' had gone; this one refused to leave, so that a return had to be made to Manston—but not before the Beaufort had received a severe mauling from the trigger-happy gunners on the coast of Ramsgate.

Much the same is true of the second machine of the delayed group. This was forced to return to base with an armed torpedo still slung under the belly and then make a wheels-up landing as it proved impossible to get the legs down. But on this unlucky day there was at least one flash of good fortune, for there was no explosion, just a jarring, skidding stop as the Bristol slithered over the frozen grass followed by the clanging fire-tender and careering 'meat-wagon'. Their services were not required.

At the controls of the third machine, the Sergeant Pilot distinguished his first operational mission by succeeding in getting his torpedo away, but it missed the target, and immediately he found himself fighting a Focke-Wulf pilot who was determined that the Coastal Command crew should die. But the running fight was drawing towards the English coast, and before the fighter pilot could administer the *coup de grâce*, it was necessary to break off the action, although the German would have had every justification in claiming it as a 'probable', for his last sight of the Beaufort showed it afire from a point under the fuselage. He could not know that the blaze would be extinguished and that, despite all the signs to the contrary, an uneventful landing would be made.

Frustrated in their first attempt to find what they believed was a 'large convoy', the pair of Beauforts that had led the departure from Manston now found themselves back there, and fresh instructions were called for. With the second machine still being serviced by the ground crew, the other machine departed a second time, and this flight was better directed, so that within a seemingly short time, with some improvement now marking the visibility, the *Gneisenau* loomed up ahead beyond the twin protective screens. The journey out had been marked by the almost continuous barking of the machine-gun at the rear, and the pilot had flown at a very low altitude to evade the fighters as far as possible and at the same time be below the worst of the anti-aircraft fire. Indeed, now that the flotilla was in sight, the seamen aboard the destroyers were involuntarily wincing as the Beaufort was eased up a few feet to miss their superstructure. Only a few seconds separated the release of the torpedo and the next attack by the fighters, so that it was no more than reflex action to pull up the nose of the powerful Bristol machine for the twin Taurus motors to send it towards the nearest cover offered by the low cloud from which the sleet had now turned to snow. Thus hidden, Pilot Officer Peter Carson was able to return his severely shot-about aircraft to base and an eventual Distinguished Flying Cross. The torpedo which it had taken so much effort to place missed the target and sank harmlessly beyond, thanks to the astute look-out system on the battle-cruiser and a skilled coxswain.

While attacks such as these were thrusting through the chaos of whirling machines over the Channel, producing such a peak of sound together with the roar of the gun-fire that they could be clearly heard on the British south-west coast, there were other sorties mounted, now in the main by Bomber Command. At about 3.15 p.m. a formation of twelve Blenheims despatched from Wattisham were noted by the Luftwaffe, several of them from No 110 Squadron making a determined assault on the *Prinz Eugen* with their loads of 250- and 500-pound bombs.

Now they came in low under the swirling cloud and were greeted by a curtain of fire that was so intense as actually to seem to hide the machines from the sight of the men in the more distant ships. They swept in now in pairs, and as the hands of the clocks slipped past the quarter-hour, a well-placed shot brought a sudden end to a Blenheim before it could even be rid of its load. Quite suddenly it appeared almost to hesitate before, in a manner seemingly without hurry, it turned away and dropped its nose slightly to reveal a banner of orange and yellow flame trailing back from the fuselage to end in a plume of black smoke before making a quickening descent into the Channel.

The lighter bombers were not the only ones in evidence for (despite the handicap that the low cloud-base imposed on the activities of aircraft capable of delivering armour-piercing bombs, any one of which could cripple the capital ships) Avro Manchesters began to appear. Among these was the formation of thirteen machines from No 207 Squadron at Bottesford in Leicester, the same type as was to be pressed into service later to sow the mouth of the River Elbe with mines in a last-ditch effort to stop the ships.

It was now about 3.30 p.m., and rising over the din above and about them the officers on the bridges of the *Scharnhorst*, now almost back with the flotilla, the *Gneisenau* and *Prinz Eugen* noticed a new outbreak of firing from the escort forming the outer screen. Clearly this was not the sound of exploding bombs but the more rhythmic sound of gunfire, the exchange of which announced that the British destroyers were now on the scene. The appearance of this new naval force changed the nature of the battle to some extent, for the best way of dealing with the intruders (apart from the attempts to sink them by gunfire) was by the use of aircraft, and thus it was that bombers with Luftwaffe markings appeared on the scene, in some cases flying almost alongside their RAF counterparts.

Meanwhile, back at the RAF bases preparations were being followed for another attack by torpedo-carrying Bristol Beauforts, this time from No 42 Squadron normally based at Leuchars in Fife. They had been ordered south only that morning. Normally this unit could muster twenty-two machines, but at that particular time only fourteen were serviceable, and of these three were without torpedoes. At the time this caused little concern, for their destination was North Coates, where the remainder could be loaded with the necessary weapons.

The original order had been for these aircraft to come down to the base in Norfolk as early as 8th February, but the move had been prevented by the weather. Despite this, when they had finally taken off four days later, it does not seem to have crossed the mind of anyone in charge that this same weather could defeat the whole operation of the attack, despite the fact that at least in Coastal Command an effort was being made to introduce some pattern of organization into the measures against the ships instead of what in effect amounted to individual attacks carried out often by small groups or perhaps single aircraft.

Even so, once again the weather triumphed, and the snow

that had fallen in the night had made it impossible for the Beauforts to land at North Coates. But it was a simple matter to divert them to Coltishall, which, although perfectly capable of receiving the machines on its cleared surface, suffered from a major drawback; this was a fighter station and in consequence had no torpedoes in its armoury. However, it was confidently believed that this would present only a small problem for it was easily possible for these to be brought to the fighter base by road, and to do this there was even proper provision, for there existed a Mobile Torpedo Servicing Unit which, with the assistance of the civil police, would make short work of the 150 miles between the two stations.

8

Eleventh Hour

For the few who saw the convoy setting off from the vicinity of Grimsby, it provided a moment's cinema-like excitement as it made its stately progress over the ice-bound roads with its motor-cycle outriders, bulky with their winter clothing against the February blast and giving an air of unreality with their frost-bespangled goggles and warnings shrilling on the winter air. In truth it was more theatrical than it was possible to judge at the time and certainly no more in conclusion than a dramatic charade, for so slow was the progress of the Mobile Unit (later to have its inefficiency hung for ever about its neck by the appellation of 'Immobile Unit') that the Nazi flotilla had almost reached the safety of German home waters when finally it entered the gates of the fighter station. Thus the decision taken long before seemed justified, that the Beauforts of No 42 Squadron wait no longer for the unarmed machines but that those already charged with torpedoes be sent against the target without delay. By now more than 2½ hours had already been frittered away while every moment in the Channel saw the flotilla a little nearer safety.

At last the nine Beauforts were airborne and heading for Kent. Manston had been instructed to expect them thirty-five minutes later, and they were to rendezvous there with a group of Hudsons from No 407, a Canadian squadron which was to provide a diversion by attacking the ships with bombs, thus allowing the torpedo-bombers a better chance of success, while fighters from Spitfire squadrons protected the whole.

For once everything went almost exactly according to plan, and all the machines detailed for the strike arrived as scheduled only to find that the idea of secrecy had now gained such a hold that no one was telling anyone about anything, and the arrival of the machines caused a surprise at Manston.

A further half hour was now wasted, during which the whole force circled, oblivious of the attempts to contact them from the base, before the Beaufort leader took his formation (further depleted when two machines became bogged down at Colti-shall) out towards the sea with five of the Canadian pilots. tagging on behind, leaving six technically obeying orders and waiting in the circuit. But in this case the Service maxim of 'Always obey the last order' only resulted in their having to return to their own base thirty minutes later, before the fuel ran out, thus preventing their reaching Bircham Newton.

Despite this chapter of inefficiency, things augured well for the Coastal Command machines, except for the cardinal flaw that so great was the need for secrecy now felt to be that orders made no mention of what the target was supposed to be, the description being couched only in vague terms that the attack was to be delivered on "a convoy"—putting one strongly in mind of the vapid wording of General Airey at Balaclava, eighty-eight years before, which had sent a large proportion of the Light Brigade to purposeless death.

It was almost 4 p.m. when they arrived over the flotilla, having navigated finally to the spot picked out by the muzzle-flashes of the guns of the ships from Harwich which had been piercing the murk. By that time the weather had taken a turn for the worse, with visibility rapidly diminishing. In fact the rain that was now steadily falling from a cloud-base in places no more than 450 feet above sea level was in fact something of an advantage once the ships had been found, for although con-ditions such as these hampered the fighters, they gave ample cover to torpedo and bombing aircraft. The latter were still being despatched, and at about this time the latest was over the fleet in the form of Hampdens of No 455 Squadron, later to be joined by further waves of Bristol Blenheim and Wellingtons.

By now British destroyers were in the thick of the fight, and while fire was exchanged with these, the German vessels had to contend with the full weight of the new bombing-force claimed by sources in Berlin at a later date to consist of a grand total of fifty-two machines. These came in to attack singly, not as a concerted force, with the *Prinz Eugen*, the *Gneisenau* and the destroyer *Z-29* receiving the brunt of the punishment. However, so great was the confusion that the British *Mackay* also received the full quota of bombs from one of the Hampdens which then turned its attention to *Worcester*, the crew no doubt puzzled and suspicious at the lack of defensive fire from the ships that they were ignorant they had misidentified.

However, the real enemy vessels were throwing up a murderous curtain of fire in their defence, and survivors recall above all else the din of the engagement. The staccato bark of the 37- and 105-millimetre anti-aircraft guns had now merged into a continuous roar, whose intensity increased as each fresh attacker came in with its load. Above this came the regular, musical clank of the spent cases falling on the armoured decks, accompanied by the orders screamed above the cacophony. With heads down, as if for additional protection, so that the rear shields of their steel helmets touched the collars of their greatcoats, the gunners stumbled and cursed on the narrow slippery decks and took what cover the shields afforded.

Then, quite suddenly, the picture changed, and one of the Hampdens became the momentary centre of attention as the strange note from one of the twin motors pierced the mindsickening din. Flames began to sweep back from the nacelle, but the machine continued on its way with seeming unconcern. A few moments later the position was changed again. The fire had obviously taken hold in the wing, and a great plume of smoke was trailing an oily stain across the sky as the machine lost height. As if eager to have its end over and done with, the British bomber rushed now with increasing speed towards the waves and struck them in a fountain of water so that it was lost from sight and was never seen again.

But if the RAF bombers were turning the fading day into a hell on the Nazi ships, the same was true of the British vessels that were now present in force. Luftwaffe reconnaissance machines had been detailed as part of 'Operation Thunderbolt' to keep the Home Fleet under continuous surveillance, and now bombing-units were despatched from the coast of northern France to deal with it. Thus it was that Dorniers and Heinkels, operating for the most part singly or in small units, often no more than a *Kette*, were seen to be flying almost alongside their British foes. It had now become that much easier for the aircraft crews on both sides to see this paradox with their own eyes, for the cloud-base had lifted by some 200 feet, although the horizontal visibility at sea level had now reduced in places to as little as half a mile; the rain that had earlier been falling fairly lightly had now increased and was sweeping across the open decks of the ships in great visible walls of water, driven by the sharp February wind.

In conditions such as these it is no surprise that both sides were as easily capable of mistakes as the other, and in the same way as the Hampden had straddled friendly vessels a little earlier in the afternoon, there is on record the attempted bombing of the destroyer *Hermann Schömann* by a Dornier 217.

It is only writers of fiction and theatrical drama who invest warfare with a counterfeit glamour, and it seems that some branches of the Armed Services come in for a greater share of this than others. The imagined cleanliness of fighting in the air is as much a fiction as any other: it is just that the introduction of machines into combat has tended to encapsulate the protagonists so that each may take false comfort from the imagined belief that he is destroying a machine—no more; the appearance of a human being from a stricken tank or a doomed aeroplane always comes as something of a mental jar to the victor.

In reality there is no difference between the aircraft crew that seeks to sink a ship and the commando who silently strangles or knifes his victim. It is just that, unlike his earth-bound brother, the pilot or bomb-aimer is not splashed with the other's blood and does not see his eyes bulge as he threshes and claws at the air. The flyer may well be condemning many men, as human in every way as himself, to a hideous death in scalding steam, to dismembering or worse while fully conscious or the perhaps equally terrible slow demise that comes stealthily to a man lost and alone in a vast unfriendly sea as he becomes slowly more numbed with cold until finally the power to reason is humanely taken from his brain. Men freshly blinded have been known to run, crazed with horror and pain, like mad animals, across the deck of a ship slowly tilting as it lists and slippery with blood and water, blundering into boats and davits in the darkness until they fling themselves deliberately into the sea after a shipping-strike by aircraft. Mercifully the airman can attack in this way again and again, for he does not see the result of his handiwork and at the back of his mind cherishes the myth of invincibility until perhaps an unlucky day when the vanguard of death penetrates his own capsule.

The Beaufort aircraft that now bore down on the Nazi flotilla were therefore no more than instruments guided to destroy the floating machines below.

It was now around four o'clock on a winter's afternoon, and the light was beginning to fade so that there is little wonder in the fact that the nine Coastal Command machines had lost their Hudson escort that was supposed to provide a diversionary attack with bombs. Now there was nothing for it but to deliver the strike alone. The formation was consequently divided into two parts, six coming in from the starboard side while three concentrated on the port quarters.

Unfortunately, after all the waiting and confusion the attack was to be something of a fiasco, as already stated. The British destroyer force was now in the vicinity, and a further case of misidentification took place when three of the Beauforts were seen making low, careful approaches on the vessels from Harwich that were now attempting to withdraw. No hits were made. Of the remaining six machines from Leuchars, two were unable to deliver any form of attack since one flew into the deepening cloud and failed to find the target on emerging, while the other suffered a malfunction of the torpedo release-gear and had to withdraw.

Despite the heavy barrage that was being sent up from the capital ships, the final four Beauforts made a determined attempt to drop their missiles accurately, and when they had turned away, all appeared to be running strongly.

It was now necessary for the machines to fight their way out, and the enormity of the problem is shown by the discovery later on that the inability of the machine to get its torpedo away earlier in the attack was due to damage sustained in several runs over the target.

As the gunfire died away, the fighters came on once more. Two Messerschmitt 109s flashed across the path of one Beaufort and then banked sharply round to come up on the tail of the British machine. The sound of the rear gun was now almost continuous, and as more fighters weighed in, a heavy encounter developed. One of the coastal aircraft sustained twelve hits in a matter of minutes, including a deep gash torn in the skin of the tailplane and a large portion knocked from an airscrew blade. In the confusion and the fading light it was difficult to see with any clarity just what was going on, although, at the same moment as a temporary lift in the cloud afforded a glimpse of the Dutch coast in the distance, one of the single-seaters was seen to be going down out of control, with smoke streaming from the engine, and one of the crew of another Beaufort claimed to have seen a ship with a pronounced list blazing furiously from the bows.

Meanwhile it still seemed that the surest way of stopping the ships lay in torpedo attacks and more Coastal Command machines were flung into the affray in accordance with a pre-arranged plan that had earmarked the Beauforts of No 86 Squadron at St Eval to counter a possible break-out into the Atlantic Ocean. Now they were ordered eastward but failed to arrive until after 2 p.m. With a repeat of the dreadful confusion at Coltishall, it was not until a further 2½ hours had been wasted that the dozen machines were waiting over Manston for their fighter escort. None came, so it was decided to press on alone, and they finally arrived over the former reported position of the flotilla nearly three-quarters of an hour later. The enemy was now far to the north, and so the formation contented itself by firing at a group of minesweepers before setting course for base. There was no alternative, for by now the light was so poor that it was at times impossible to distinguish between sea and sky. It is believed that this was the reason for the disappearance of two machines from the formation. They simply vanished without trace, and it is assumed that they flew into the sea and sank.

At much the same moment as this was happening, Admiral Ciliax was in communication with Luftwaffe chiefs, requesting additional fighter protection for the ships, as it was felt that the fading light was now aiding those aircraft which managed to find the flotilla, since it only wanted one to slip through the protective screens undetected for the *Scharnhorst, Gneisenau* or *Prinz Eugen* to receive its death-blow. In view of the lateness of the hour the situation obviously required the ordering back into the battle area of the night fighters that had been stood down for most of the day at bases on the Dutch coast. It was not long after that the ships' crews strained their eyes upwards and noted that the single-seaters which had maintained the daylight vigil were now augmented by Messerschmitt 110s of the *Nachtjagdver-bände*.

Despite the fading light of the chill February day, the attacks continued. Overhead there were more Handley Page Hampdens and further Bristol Beauforts, some of which had only now managed to find the targets after a long search. Meanwhile one of the bombers was seen immediately above the *Prinz Eugen*, audaciously ignoring the fire from the ships and the fighters that were in hot pursuit. The fire from below faltered since the big ugly bomber was obviously above the pre-determined range of the guns and easy meat for the Luftwaffe pilots. It was a moment of cold courage, while the bomber-aimer lay on his stomach behind the transparent nose giving final directions over the intercom to his pilot. The two gunners at the back, above and below the boom-like rear fuselage, could do little more than hose away with their rifle-calibre Vickers guns at the Messerschmitts behind, now joined in the distance by Focke-Wulf 190s, a type so new that some of the British crews had never encountered them before. They had squandered valuable seconds, sometimes with fatal results, hesitating whether this was friend or foe.

In a series of almost textbook attacks the single-seaters now came on with guns blazing brightly in the poor light and then peeled away for the following machine to put in a burst. The result was a foregone conclusion. Almost over the cruiser a quick tongue of flame swiftly took hold of the bomber that swung away and plunged into the sea to the sound of cheers of relief from the crew of the vessel it had so recently threatened.

Hardly had the waves swallowed up this new victim than another Hampden appeared. Lower than his colleague, the altitude placed him easily within the range of the guns. Time and again it seemed that the curtain of fire that at times hid the bomber from view must have accounted for it, but as the ships pitched and rolled, the men aboard were able to see it still there, coming inexorably on as if incapable of suffering destruction. Now the machine was over the destroyer *Z-29* which had been in the thick of the fighting for so long, and suddenly the luck that had attended the Hampden deserted it. One moment it was holding serenely on its course, the next it was unrecognizable as an aeroplane at all, but just a flaming cross in the sky. Inside the pilot was humanely dead, felled by a cannon shell exploding behind his head so that the blood spurted out and obscured the inside of the canopy with a red curtain that could be seen as a bright splash of crimson by the final fighter of a group which had been attracted by the fire from patrol at a higher altitude.

While all round the noise of battle rolled, there was hardly a pause before the gunners who had so recently slain the bomber saw before them a new development. There at low altitude was one of the single Beauforts. Despite the heavy and accurate fire that the ships were sending up, the pilot had obviously digested well those operational instructions that stated that, under poor lighting "conditions of visibility will govern the approach", which should "be made in a shallow dive or at dropping-height". Some way from the *Gneisenau*, ploughing ahead and sending up a great swathe of white water from her bows as she did so, the torpedo was seen to fall away from the machine. In a moment it was in the water with the familiar splash and could be seen clearly running below the surface. There was a flurry of activity on board the battle-cruiser, and the wake swung away in a graceful curve the manœuvre was sufficient, and the surface runner passed harmlessly by the huge wall of the grey-camouflaged hull. It was a movement not unknown to the men watching on the *Prinz Eugen*, for her gunners had cursed the coxswain who had time and again ruined their aim that day—a day that was not to pass without the honourable indignity of fifteen men toiling under the guns on the afterdeck steering her by muscle-power alone after one torpedo-attack by Coastal Command. Despite this handicap the day was well advanced when a signal was seen from the cruiser and noted on the *Gneisenau* ahead: "Hanging on to you 5,620 yards starboard astern."

It was then that there descended a great calm, almost for the first time that day since the two Spitfires had blundered on the capital ships and their escort that morning. For ten blissful minutes the flotilla steamed on for all the world as if taking part in a peacetime exercise. Except for the comforting presence of the fighter umbrella, the sky that had so recently been torn with fighting planes and blasted by shell-burst was now empty, and orders on the vessels that had been shrieked a short time before could be heard delivered in a normal military voice.

The last wave of bombers had been one of the most difficult to

A preserved, airworthy specimen of a Fairy Swordfish gives a frail appearance that belies the great strength of this design.

Second from left in this group is Lieutenant-Commander Esmond, who was posthumously awarded the Victoria Cross for leading the attack by Swordfish aircraft. On the extreme right is Leading Airman A. L. 'Ginger' Johnson DSM, who was killed in the attack defending Edgar Lee's machine.

The sight of a Spitfire shape similar to this announced to the Nazi ships' crews that the escape had been discovered. Flying Officer Kenneth Campbell, who won a posthumous Victoria Cross on 6th April 1941 while attempting to torpedo *Gneisenau* from a Bristol Beaufort of No 22 Squadron numbered N1016.

Group-Captain Francis Victor Beamish DSO and Bar, DFC, AFC, is seen here at a slightly earlier period as a Wing-Commander, wearing a forage-cap in the centre of the group.

A 15-inch long-range gun showing the size of this type of weapon.

Shell-bursts on the right fall near to some destroyers forming part of the inner protective screen.

An escort vessel (on the right) leads the three vessels up the Channel through a local clearance in the weather. The mast of *Prinz Eugen* may just be made out between the two battle-cruisers on the left.

HMS *Worcester*, one of the elderly British warships that made up Destroyer Flotillas 16 and 21. She was extensively damaged in the action but managed to reach port without assistance.

Captain Mark Pizey was in command of the combined flotilla aboard HMS *Campbell*, and it was to this vessel that the captains came to discuss plans before setting out.

Before distinguishing herself by somewhat poor gunnery in pursuit of the Royal Navy MTBs, it had been claimed that the *Friedrich Ihn* had saved the capital ships by drawing the fire of the Dover coastal batteries.

Anti-aircraft guns on *Prinz Eugen* firing, it has been claimed, at torpedo-bombers early in the attempt to attack the flotilla.

Nazi crews were to remember the worst part of the action, when ships had to heave to after *Scharnhorst* struck a mine. Here some gunners scan the sky while an escort vessel stands by.

The *Gneisenau* as seen from the starboard rail of *Prinz Eugen* during the terminal stage of the voyage on Friday 13th February.

Safe at last in Wilhelmshaven, the crew of *Scharnhorst* line her rails and find it easy to smile for the camera after their ordeal of the previous days.

deal with, not due to any improvements in tactics on the part of the RAF but because now, as the day was almost through, the gunners and crews had received no rest or respite from their duties since before the raid on Brest that had bidden fair to wreck all the plans the night before.

The force that had carried out the latest attack had been a mixed one, and the Nazis were not slow to realize that this must indicate the state of unpreparedness that the lightning break-out had found amongst their enemies. With over thirty Spit-fires, their strength dissipated by being sent in small for-mations, the final wave had been formed of forty-one machines, all bombers. The larger number had been Wellingtons, nine-teen in all, while a further sixteen had been equally divided between four-engined bombers, Short Stirlings and Handley Page Halifax machines, a type that had been withdrawn from daylight assaults on land targets following the last attack on Brest at the close of 1941. The final component of this force had been contributed by six of the ubiquitous Bristol Blenheims. These, attacking from 11,000 feet, had claimed 'possible hits' from three of their number, but the Intelligence summary issued the following day is vague on the question of what vessel is claimed to have been hit and the extent of the damage, contenting itself with the comment that the crews "did not observe results".

The unexpected tranquillity was not to last long, however, for, a little more than ten minutes after the sound of the last gun had died away on the wet depressing afternoon air, a signal was received by Vice-Admiral Ciliax that the *Gneisenau* would be falling back. This was due entirely to a technical fault that had caused her to reduce revolutions on the starboard shaft so that for the first time that day the cruiser now held the intermediate position with a battle-cruiser ahead and aft.

It was only a little later that the bogey of technical mal-function struck once more, when the *Z-29*, to which the Vice-Admiral and his staff had transferred earlier in the day, showed signs of trouble in the port engine. It was obviously out of the question for the Commander-in-Chief to remain with a vessel that might at any moment, when the attacks were resumed, become a 'sitting duck', and so, with the aid of a cutter in a sea that was now becoming increasingly rough, a second transfer was made, this time to the *Hermann Schömann*. It was now approaching 6 p.m., and the light of the winter day was fading fast when, with one of the ironies which seemed to mark the day on both sides, the Admiral turned on his uncomfortable seat a few feet above the waves, just in time to see pass the majestic bulk of *Scharnhorst* which he had quitted earlier in the day following the incident with the mine, now speeding along with a good bow wave, her captain intent on rejoining the main body of the ships before dark.

The short-lived peace was over now, and the final remnants of the bombing-force of Wellingtons was causing the guns of the capital ships and their escort to erupt into a new thunder of hate as they came in to drop their loads. In a few moments two had been accounted for either by the gunners or by the mixed protection of day and night fighters, and sent into the freezing sea to join the masses of aluminium wreckage, remains of the aircraft from both sides that now and again floated past, which could be seen clearly from the decks.

The final bomber assault had been the last of more than two hundred machines that the Command had despatched that fateful day since a little before noon, but the vast majority of these had failed to find the ships and had either brought their loads home or selected alternative targets.

By now, three quarters of an hour after the Nazi commander and his depleted staff had taken up their positions in the new flagship, the darkness of the winter day was complete. But plainly the RAF had no intention of allowing their potential prizes to escape if that was possible, and Coastal Command had shortly before sent off a pair of Beaufighters to shadow the force. At about 6 p.m. one of these reported sighting what was taken to be the *Scharnhorst* with an escort of six destroyers at a position about 15 miles south-west of Den Helder. As the hours of darkness wore on, further aircraft were sent off to keep the flotilla under observation, and a Wellington, a Whitley and two Consolidated Catalina flying-boats shared the surveillance.

During this time there were also more active measures being taken to thwart the enemy plans, and an intensive operation was even then taking place to mine the course that the vessels were now inevitably to take. In consequence the hours of darkness were still punctuated over the Channel and beyond as aircraft left to mine the whole of the sea area ahead of the Nazi squadron right up to the estuary of the Elbe and the German Bight. Although no major actions were to take place, the night fighter force was completely alive to what was going on and made contact with the minelayers whenever possible during the night.

That the measures being taken by Coastal Command were wise ones was shown at about 8 p.m., when, just as the operation seemed to have settled down to a conclusion of watch-like precision, there was a brilliant flash in the February sky and those on board *Gneisenau* were aware of the jolt that comes from a heavy underwater explosion. The battle-cruiser was alone at the time, having just a little earlier weathered a squall, but was making progress again at 28 knots near to the Frisians, where the marker-boats still clustered to show the way.

Experienced men exchanged glances and tersely told the new hands what the awesome sound meant: they had struck a mine —in fact, one of those which had been sown by the RAF earlier in the day. All the engines went suddenly quiet, the middle one as a direct result of the explosion, the others shut down on the orders of Captain Fein until the damage could be inspected. In the tense moments that followed there was a pregnant quiet on the vessel as she slowly drifted with the tide, and then the repair-parties emerged to give their report. Although there was certainly a hole in the starboard side, the damage was not serious, and once the gap had been made good with a water-proof mat and plug, they could be on the move once more if the speed was kept down to a cautious 10 knots and the pumps kept going. Half an hour later found the *Gneisenau* making progress despite a failure of the navigational aids. Meanwhile the *Prinz Eugen* was searching for the battle-cruiser in the blackness.

Thirty minutes after *Gneisenau* was creeping along again, *Scharnhorst* was making good progress off the coast of Holland, and such was her speed that the crew, although weary now, were finding time to eat and exchange talk. After a further half hour the atmosphere had completely changed and was now almost one of confident ebullience. It was at this moment that a violent explosion shook the vessel so that men standing about in groups were sent spinning; to the accompaniment of a heavy boom the lights flickered out and the electrical equipment failed. It was not Captain Hoffmann's lucky day. His vessel had survived one mine in daylight only to strike another in the hours of darkness.

Once more there was an agonizing wait while the engineers groped to discover the worst with the aid of hand-lamps. That it was serious was obvious. A great deal of water had filled her, giving a list to starboard; there could be no power except from auxiliary sources for some time; much damage was done to the instruments, and the rudder had suffered, but despite this dismal catalogue it was by no means grave.

In spite of the cold of the winter night, the men who toiled in the heavy atmosphere between the decks stripped off as the temperature within rose. In the blackness, with only the glimmer of lamps, they worked till they could hardly stand, but they still carried on, so that at about 10.15 p.m. the hum of two of the three motors could be heard once more. The port one was useless, but she could make progress at 14 knots on the starboard and middle engines. Ahead the *Hermann Schömann*, like a guardian angel, led the way to Wilhelmshaven, while the search by *Prinz Eugen* for *Gneisenau* was also ended. But the time was not one for congratulation or complacency. The unfriendly night was now at its darkest; the waters through which they sailed were sown with mines, they knew not where, and haven in a German port was still far distant.

9

Sea Wolves

If the almost unceasing harassment of the Nazi squadron by aircraft had been the only problem to be dealt with, apart from those of a technical nature, the dash of the *Scharnhorst, Gneisenau* and *Prinz Eugen* past what had once been the holiday beaches of south-east England would have been difficult enough. But there was far more to contend with, as was to be expected just as certainly in 1942 as in 1588, when another audacious enemy was in the Channel: the size of the problem was nothing less than the Royal Navy.

The destroyer *Campbell*, under the command of Captain C. T. M. Pizey, and that of Lieutenant-Commander Alexander constituted the 21st Flotilla out of Harwich. With this force and from the same home port was the 16th Destroyer Flotilla made up of *Mackay* carrying the Commander, Captain J. P. Wright, *Worcester* under Lieutenant-Commander Colin Coates, *Whitshed* with Lieutenant-Commander W. A. Juniper and *Walpole* with Lieutenant-Commander John Eadon on the bridge. As we have seen in Chapter Seven, all these vessels were more than twenty years old, but whatever deficiencies were imposed by age, they were to some extent balanced by the preparedness that was (and, despite the politicians, still is) a watchword in the Royal Navy, for the engine-rooms were permanently at five minutes readiness, and the officers and men slept in their clothes so that they could immediately sail for the battle-area. There the small and fast motor-torpedo boats were expected to slow or halt the capital ships in concert with the Swordfish attacks in the manner of the tactics which had accounted for the *Bismarck*, so that the *coup de grâce* could then be given by larger vessels or possibly the Dover guns on the South Foreland.

The destroyers had already been at sea that morning in the

cold, depressing blackness that marks the hours before dawn on a winter's day, to take part in a practice shoot under the protection of half-a-dozen Hunt-class destroyers armed with a formidable array of anti-aircraft artillery.

Part of the exercise was over, and it was approaching noon when the signal was received that the enemy vessels were close at hand. As the engines sent a surge of power through each of the destroyers while they changed course and built up their speed, lunch was served on the mess decks. Meanwhile, Mark Pizey had to decide the swiftest course along which to direct his helmsman, and the one that seemed certain to take his force directly to the estimated enemy position lay on the opposite side of a British minefield. It seemed to him that there was no alternative. His duty was clear. Orders were given for the flotillas to proceed through the death-sown sea.

In fact the danger was not as great as it seemed, for there existed a narrow area of no more than a mile in width that was supposed to be clear of mines, but the trip was believed to be hazardous enough, for there was the ever-present danger of floating mines torn from their moorings by the winter's storms. Even so, very careful navigation was called for, and to negotiate the passage the destroyers were strung out in a long line astern with *Walpole* last, a wise decision for shortly after 1 p.m. it became obvious that the elderly engines could not stand the pace at 28 knots, when it was reported that the bearings were running hot. Scarcely had this fact been signalled to Mark Pizey, who ordered her captain to return to Harwich, than what appeared to be Bristol Blenheims appeared on the horizon.

As the flight came nearer, it was obvious that they were certainly not the friendly bombers from the Filton factory that they appeared to be, but instead similar-looking Junkers 88s which immediately dropped their loads all round the destroyers without managing to hit or damage any of them, although some fell too close for comfort to Wright's *Mackay*. What, in the circumstances, was more serious was that the element of surprise had now gone, and the look-outs on the capital ships would be on the alert for the destroyer's appearance. As the five continued at high speed through the narrow channel, there followed other sporadic attacks, one in the manner of the day by a British bomber which seemed to single out *Worcester*. This was the brush with the Hampden.

Half an hour after this distinct blips began to show up on the radar on *Campbell*'s bridge, first a pair together and then a single one, the latter being *Scharnhorst* under way once more after the encounter with the first mine.

It was approaching a quarter to four in the afternoon when Captain Pizey signalled his intention to close in to the attack, for the radar-plots had shown the enemy only 9 miles ahead. With the traditional wishes for 'Good Luck' at their end, *Campbell* raced in the direction of the *Gneisenau*.

At that exact moment in time the crew of the battle-cruiser had other things on their minds, for they were being subjected to a determined assault by the Royal Air Force in the form of Coastal Command's Bristol Beauforts so that some were surprised when the winking of muzzle-flashes in the gloom and the explosion of a shell near to the waterline announced that a surface force had arrived and had beaten its way through the protective screen of E-boats.

Two miles astern of *Gneisenau* speeded the *Prinz Eugen*, and the two swung their guns in unison as the British flotillas strung out on a parallel course. It seemed that the smaller ships must be doomed, for fire was being exchanged at scarcely more than 3,000 yards.

Gneisenau, in the lead, came in for the greatest concentration of fire from the destroyers, and both *Campbell* and *Vivacious* now turned together and discharged their torpedoes simultaneously, although the latter had just survived a similar assault from an unidentified Nazi destroyer that had suddenly loomed out of the mist which seemed to make unnecessary the smoke—screen still being laid. Having delivered their attack and finding it impossible to observe the results, the two destroyers swung away into the murk. This immediately brought suspicion into the minds of the officers on the bridge of the Nazi ships for a manœuvre of this nature surely meant, they believed, that the shadowy shapes that were to be seen at the limit of vision were not more destroyers but cruisers.

It was now that the attention of the battle fell on *Worcester*, for (perhaps to make up for the loss of the *Walpole* which, even then, had managed to limp back to port), Colin Coats on the bridge of the next vessel in line took the 'Saucebottle' in to within even shorter range of the 11-inch guns of the leading Nazi ship. In addition to this, the destroyer was also the centre of attention from the gunners on the larger vessels that formed the outer screen at a range of some 2,500 yards, so that it was in reality only a matter of time before doom overtook the British destroyer, although the violent evasive action that the Nazi ships were being forced to take to keep out of the way of the torpedoes from HMS *Campbell* and *Vivacious* was certainly contributing to the problems of the Nazi gun-layers.

At this point the sea about the *Worcester*, now considerably less than 2 miles distant from the larger ships, seemed to erupt and boil with the fall of the shells; close in to the vessel herself fountains of water were hurled into the air higher than the masthead. By this time the range had diminished to a point where, with little more than a mile between the heavy guns of the battle-cruiser and the target, there was no longer any need to do more than fire directly at the destroyer; any elevation would now only ensure a miss.

A sound was then heard which for the moment blotted out all others, and at the same second the destroyer shook from bow to stern with the impact.

Torpedoes are fired from a ship of this type from the bridge, but there was provided a means by which they could be alternatively sent on their way by a gunner below. Almost at the same moment as the first shell (the cause of the explosion) had struck the destroyer, the order to fire the torpedoes had been given, but the hit had carried away all the bridge communications so that, although the officer aloft thumbed his trigger as a reflex-action, it was actually from lower down that the 'fish' leapt into the water. The few who had the self-control to note how things were going turned to more urgent tasks in despair as they saw the risks taken in bringing *Worcester* in so close go to waste as the missiles left their trail on a harmless course parallel to that of the target vessels.

As one will, a seaman looked at his watch and noted that it was ten minutes to four in the afternoon, and at the precise moment that he did so, there was a second and greater explosion than the first, so close to it that there were those between decks that remember the combined report as an unbroken roll as if of nearby thunder.

This time two shells had found their mark and had ripped, as if through paper, a massive rent in the steel plates from a point mid-way over the deck to somewhere below the waterline. All the effort and sacrifice had been in vain, although it was probably as much due to the evasive action that the Nazi cruiser was taking from the rain of bombs which the RAF was delivering at the same moment that the strike was abortive.

Worcester was now helpless and for ten minutes drifted on the swell, at one time without the benefit of her engines, swinging round through 180 degrees so that she presented a broadside target to the enemy whose gunners could wish for nothing better: four more hits were scored from the two capital ships. A huge hole was blown in the port bow, and another gaped below the bridge. There was no longer a mast, and two boiler-rooms were holed and in chaos while a fire raged in the paint-locker.

As the destroyer drifted further off and became lost in the smoke from this and from that laid by the enemy ships to provide cover, those who could watched from the vantage-points provided by their own ships. They noted that there was a perceptible reluctance to right herself from each roll, brought about by the quantity of water that had been shipped. Realizing that this placed his vessel in a position where she might capsize at any moment, Colin Coates gave the preliminary order, "Prepare to abandon ship," not knowing that by doing so he was bringing about a change in Admiralty policy. Such was the din and confusion on board that the complete wording was not heard by some, who passed on a shortened version to the effect that the order to "abandon ship" had been given. That it seemingly had was no surprise. Carley floats and rafts were tossed over the side, and the wounded were lowered on to them, although the task was increasingly difficult as the sea was becoming rougher.

It was the work of a moment for the Commander to look down from his wrecked bridge, where he had survived as if by a miracle without hurt, and to issue and order righting the situation, but by now the swell had taken some of the rafts and floats too far from *Worcester*'s side, and the men huddled on them looked up in apprehension as two new shapes loomed out of the smoke.

This time the tormented sailors were in luck, for a moment at least, as the new arrivals were none other than *Vivacious* and *Campbell*, the former having discharged her torpedoes almost half an hour previously, when they had passed ahead of the target without causing any harm. Then, just as succour was in sight, the engine-room telegraph on board HMS *Campbell* signalled full speed astern in a violent avoiding-action, and the wash flung the men into the water where the bitter cold threatened their lives anew until it was possible for the two destroyers to take them aboard.

Meanwhile, the engineers on the stricken *Worcester* had been working wonders in the close confines below decks and had toiled to some purpose, for it now became obvious that the tow-line that was even then being prepared on *Campbell* was not needed since sufficient steam had been raised on the other destroyer for it to be possible for a slow return to be made to Harwich, in common later with *Vivacious* and *Campbell*, since all vessels that had discharged their torpedoes were ordered back to port.

The light was rapidly fading now, and as the long journey home was begun, every effort was being made to lighten the ship, for by this time the battle had passed, and a great quiet had descended after the engulfing din of only a short time before. However, there still existed a danger of the ship going down at any moment into the freezing ocean. There was still plenty of water in one of the boiler-rooms, and though a second was unusable, the third was in working order; it was herein that their chief hope of reaching Harwich lay, although that boiler might at any moment fail them, as it was necessary for it to be run on sea water from which the salt could quickly choke it into failure.

By now *Worcester* was alone, and although all the able-bodied officers and men were bent on nursing the ship on its painful way, it was only too clear to those who could momentarily pause and look around that their numbers were depleted, some lost when the order was misinterpreted, others dead or in the little groups of wounded amongst whom the ship's doctor was still moving, slithering about on the rolling deck made more treacherous by the quantities of blood that ran from side to side with the moment of the sea.

Whitshed and *Mackay* had also hove to, a little further off in the protective group that had gathered about the stricken *Worcester*, but now that these had dispersed, the four were making their individual ways home, which they finally reached about midnight. It had been a long and terrible day, and the early-morning departure to take part in the firing-exercise seemed very far off indeed. Life on a warship sees no neat divisions into day and night with individuals allotted to one period or the other; during time of war, if seamen are alive and on duty, then they work, irrespective of what time of day it may be. It was so now, for the home-coming of *Whitshed*, *Mackay*, *Worcester* and *Campbell* was to be of but short duration, only long enough to replenish the essentials and take on fresh ammunition and torpedoes before putting to sea once more to hunt for the escaping foe.

This, Admiral Ciliax knew, must be the pattern of events, for he was an experienced and shrewd officer, and it was in the light of this belief that his apprehension, reflected in the conduct of those under him, was at its greatest when the capital ships had been forced to halt in the minefields. If either of them had been discovered by the hunting destroyers, it could so easily, he knew, be a repeat of the saga of the last hours of the *Bismarck*. In fact, the luck of the day still seemed determined to protect the fugitives, for although the four destroyers sought their quarry throughout the night, no trace did they ever find.

Equally wasted was the effort of a further flotilla of four destroyers that had been sent from port to provide a protective escort. They failed to find the near-crippled *Worcester* in the darkness, probably because they had no idea just how slow her progress really was, since at no time was it possible to make a better speed than some 6 knots. The average rate of travel was in reality even less, for the night was not without its problems.

The first of these had arisen at a little after 7 p.m., when the water-feed to the boilers had petered out so that there was no steam for a short while; under conditions such as these the sea simply takes over a ship with a large amount of water still in the bottom of her hull. The rolling that now took place was sufficiently alarming for the order to be given again for a fresh search to jettison all movable excess weight; this time the task of stripping the ship was concentrated on the upper works where the pendulum effect of the load could at any moment completely capsize her. With steam-pressure once again restored, it was possible to limp homewards at something less than 4 knots for another two hours. But then the same thing happened afresh, and although the sea was calmer now, the perilous toil to restore the vital water-flow was resumed while the destroyer rolled in the blackness like the writhings of some grotesque sea-monster.

The *Worcester*'s crew now began to realize how cold it was, and the sea was once more beginning to be whipped into white caps of foam by a rising wind which tore at the over-black smoke from the funnel and pulled it aft in tatters like witches' hair from some nightmare picture-book. All about lay the wounded between whom the doctor and his attendant still picked their way, here and there covering a man to whom human relief had come too late; the final figures claimed that in a ship's company of 130 there were seventeen dead and twenty-seven minor casualties plus six missing and eighteen with graver hurts. In the gloomy atmosphere it seemed more and may even have been so for wartime figures were seldom completely accurate since their publication was available to friend and foe alike, and they had frequently to be gathered under difficult conditions and at short notice.

Discarding the heavy equipment had resulted in the loss of much in the way of navigational aids, and the only sure way now was to steer a course that had been obtained from HMS *Campbell* shortly before they had parted. This was merely the reversal of the journey out and therefore contained the same little flaw that it had before—it called for a passage through the minefield. If bringing a seaworthy vessel through this hazard with the necessary reduction of speed in the mile-wide lane had been difficult before, it was reckoned a thousand times more dangerous now, since the two periods when the loss of steam-pressure had necessitated the ship heaving to had proved that it was very largely only the forward motion that was keeping her afloat. Thus Captain Coates had to perform a sort of navigational balancing-act between keeping the speed down in the restricted channel through the minefield and keeping it up to ensure that the ship remained afloat. Still the little steel world ploughed on in the void of the isolating blackness.

As the hands of the clock crept to 4 a.m. on the morning of

the following Friday, the ship was as if manned by ghosts as the
seamen went silently about their work, the lightly wounded
with their colleagues, the bandages of the former giving them
the appearance of sailors in shrouds. Some had helped carry
their dead comrades to the rail, and while the First Officer read
the burial service, they were committed to the deep, one small
change in the ritual being the necessity for the destroyer to
remain on the move while this was being done, not heave to as is
usual, for to do so now could mean disaster.

Still the embattled ship limped on. To the outside world it
had vanished without trace, and there was no way in which the
truth could be told. For all that the Admiralty knew HMS
Worcester might now be at the bottom.

In London, their Lordships were made of sterner stuff. They
were seamen themselves and knew the traditions and hopes of
those who live on the ocean, and in consequence a strange order
went out from London. For some two years now England had
been a land mantled in blackness at night, for the black-out was
complete and all-enveloping. The directive then, was as surprising as it was unusual, namely that the lighthouse on the Suffolk
coast about 20 miles from Harwich at Orford Ness expose its
beam, a measure ordered to be taken on the chance that the
destroyer was in the area and required assistance.

For Lieutenant-Commander Coates on the bridge, the sight
of this beacon gave new hope and indicated that his vessel was
still on course, a fact that was confirmed just as the dreary
winter dawn began to lighten up the horizon when the look-out
reported the Sunk Light at the entrance to Harwich (not far
from the course taken today by the car-ferries to Ostend). They
were as resurrected men returned from the dead.

Almost the first sign of human life came from a Hunt-class
destroyer, from the deck of which an Aldis lamp was winking,
asking if the *Worcester* required assistance. This was declined, as
they had come thus far and were determined to make port
alone, but the message ended with a request for ambulances to
stand by. As the light improved, men on other ships in the
Harwich dock could see clearly the spectacle of the scarecrow
vessel that was limping through their midst. She was listing
heavily; what was left of the mast lay at a crazy angle, and both
funnels were shorn off short, altering her outline. The fire had

devoured a large part of the bows, and a great gaping void under the bridge rivalled the one cut by the shells in her side that was now plugged with hammocks and a collision-mat. The hull was punctured by a series of holes both large and small, through which steam escaped to rise in the cold of the February morning. The radio-room had ceased to exist, and it was obvious to the experienced eye that there had been explosions in the ammunition-lockers.

Throughout the night, despite the parlous condition of the ship, the traditions and the self-control of the Royal Navy had not been allowed to lapse. There had been no panic, and orders were given in an air of quiet confidence that upheld morale. Officers exchanged requests couched in the usual courtesies. The atmosphere was such therefore that all on board (long past the point of breakdown but now at the point of assuring their survival by the chain of discipline that ensured self-control) were going to play the part to the logical conclusion. With the ensign flying from a staff that looked suspiciously as if it normally did duty as the handle of a broom, *Worcester* was going to tie up alone.

What followed was one of those strange spontaneous ceremonies that stern and hardened fighting men will sometimes stage without embarrassment or thought of doing other than express their feelings in a manner more eloquent than words. As the destroyer struggled along, those not below decks became slowly aware that a great hooting filled the air. It was the sound of the sirens of all the ships in harbour loosing off in welcome. They did more: the shrill sounds of boatswains' pipes cut into the frosty air; from below, the men who could be spared came up to line the traditional ceremonial area of a warship, the quarterdeck, where they fell in as if on parade and cheered themselves hoarse.

Only dimly aware of what was going on about them—what with the wounds of many that were now beginning to stiffen and the lack of rest, plus the reaction now to the strain of battle—those on board the destroyer still had much to do: the ropes had to be flung down to the wailing tugs, and care had to be taken as always in the approach to Harwich, where a fickle tide can sweep a ship onto the sand-banks. As the slack was taken up on the tow, there was a sudden change in the noise of the engine-room that had dinned the ears for so long now. The men exchanged enquiring glances as to what it could be. It took them only a few seconds to realize: the oil-pump that they had nursed all night had ceased again. There was almost a humour in the situation, for it was completely irreparable.

After the burial of the dead, four of the more seriously wounded had died, and their bodies were now carried to the waiting ambulances. (For long this total of slain was publicized as the sum of those killed.) They were followed by the wounded who required hospital care, and then came the men who had been through hell unscathed, some of them with their uniforms heavy and stiff, soaked through with the blood of their less-fortunate fellows. Discipline enduring to the last, Colin Coates was the last to make for the gangway of the now empty and echoing ship. As he did so, he paused, slipped the ensign from the broomstick and rolled it up; he carried it under his arm as he followed his men to food, hot baths and rest. "The Sauce-bottle'll want a refit, I'd say," murmured a rating with an attempt at humour. If they heard him, nobody laughed; all they wanted now was sleep.

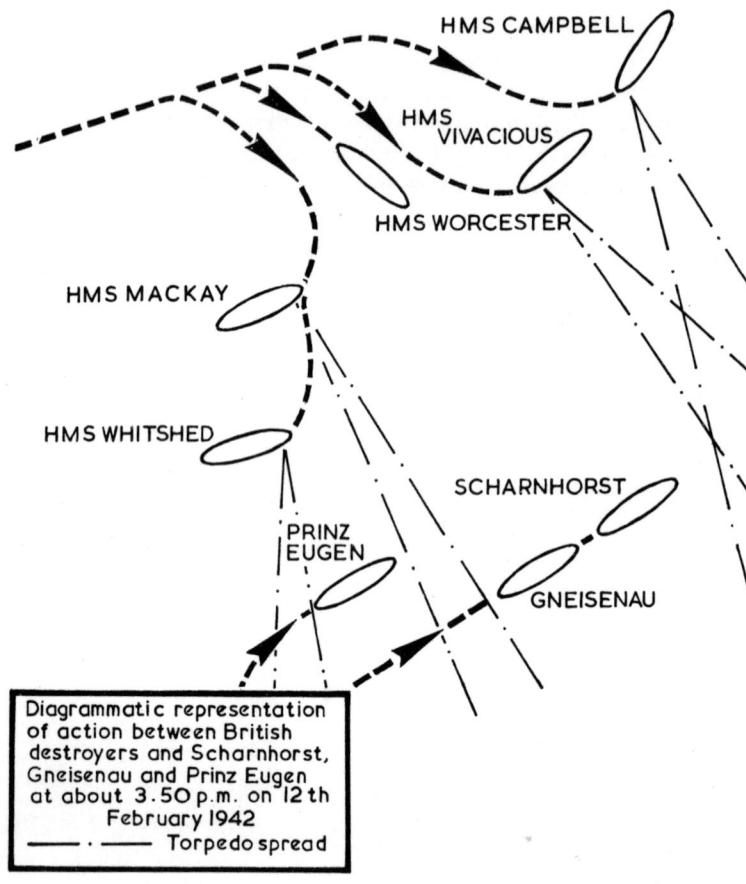

HMS CAMPBELL

HMS
VIVACIOUS

HMS WORCESTER

HMS MACKAY

HMS WHITSHED

SCHARNHORST

PRINZ
EUGEN

GNEISENAU

Diagrammatic representation
of action between British
destroyers and Scharnhorst,
Gneisenau and Prinz Eugen
at about 3.50 p.m. on 12th
February 1942
—— · —— Torpedo spread

The engagement of the Nazi squadron by British destroyers

10

Friday the 13th

Understandably there existed within the Luftwaffe a certain pride for those members who had taken part in 'Operation Cerberus', as the escape up the Channel was finally termed in Nazi military circles. But although a large section of the air arm had taken part, there were some units, even day-fighter units, that were frustrated. These had nothing to do but to sit by their radios throughout the cold day and try to imagine what was going on, all the time hoping at the backs of their minds that the next five minutes would bring the order which would send them sprinting for their narrow cockpits, swiftly buckling on their parachutes and harness before bumping across the snow-covered grass and finally roaring into the air and heading for the great and dangerous operation over the narrow sea.

For some the wait was in vain, and while the more philosophic merely shrugged their shoulders and told each other that war mostly is waiting, punctuated with moments of wild activity, their more mercurial colleagues chafed and could settle to no diversion but instead paced up and down, smoked cigarettes that were tossed away only half consumed and attempted to read magazines which failed to hold their attention.

The following day was a Friday, and the date was the 13th. Back on duty the Luftwaffe fighter crews eyed the date with suspicion. For whom would it be unlucky? Little did they realize that their British counterparts were thinking the same thoughts. But whatever the shade of their uniforms, both knew that there could be no action for them until the cold darkness of the winter's early morning gave place to light after dawn.

Release from the tension came for the fighter crews at Jever just after 9 a.m. on that fateful Friday morning. Ignorant of what the position really was in the mist-shrouded Channel, many imagined that the order to take off would at last send them to the scene of action over the capital ships. As one by one the hoods of their Messerschmitts were closed over their heads they recalled that they had heard strong rumours about the intended break since three days before, or at least they later said that they recalled the fact. If their memories were not deceiving them then, it is of historical interest, since of necessity it means that the elaborate and complex security measures were all to no avail and that even the frequent change of code-name, carried out several times before the final adoption of 'Cerberus', had failed in its intended purpose. (Within Nazi flying-circles the cover for the Channel escape had most frequently been coded 'Thunderbolt', a term that appealed much more to the alert and youthful minds of the aviators.)

As the *Kette*s winged their way out over the sea, a glance downward confirmed why some of the units had spent the previous day on the ground: now that they could view the picture beyond the smaller confines of their snow-mantled field, it was clear that the weather was determined to do its worst to frustrate them—a claim that was to be made within a short time by British circles, for the waves below were of a threatening grey-green shade with white caps, and even at low altitude the gusts of a bitter wind could be felt by the pilots.

Below loomed a small vessel, a minesweeper. As if the traditional trigger-happy gunners needed encouragement, they had now been ordered to fire at anything that flew, so that Flight-Commanders were careful to fire the recognition-signals that would ensure their safety. Almost at the same moment an exchange over the intercom alerted the pilots to the presence of shapes looming through the fog, and in a moment they materialized as British bombers.

Airmen are notoriously ignorant of the ways of the sea, but it was obvious to all that by now—if they had survived the almost unceasing British assaults of the previous day by long-range gun, destroyer, MTB, MGB, bomber, rocket-armed fighter and torpedo aircraft, including the 'mothball air force' as the Nazis were to term the Swordfish, and if the *Scharnhorst, Gneisenau* and *Prinz Eugen* had, under the protection of the overworked Luftwaffe, survived all this—they must be beyond the range of fighters and at a point where only bombers could reach them.

With thoughts along these lines half formed at the back of their pilots' minds, the Jever fighters now swept in to deal with the Blenheims. A long burst of fire from a Messerschmitt sets one motor of a bomber alight, but the target vanishes before the attack can be pressed home. An indecisive skirmish follows, but the overcast provides adequate cover for the bombers, and little damage is suffered by either side, although an Me 109 goes down on fire to make an emergency landing at an advanced airfield before the fuel runs out. The Blenheims meanwhile vanish.

Had they but known it, the elated fighter crews who had chafed their way through the previous day were, as the hands of the clock slowly ticked past 10 a.m. making no contribution to the guardianship of the capital vessels since by now the main part of the operation had been completed and the ships had successfully carried out perhaps the greatest propaganda and military success up to that time. The fateful Friday now presented a completely different picture.

On the ships the position had changed its details in many particulars, including that of the vessel from which the Vice-Admiral now flew his flag. Otto Ciliax, the 'Black Czar' of the German Navy, was no longer aboard the *Z-29*, for the oil-feed had been severed by a shell splinter. The flagship was now the *Hermann Schömann*, to which the Admiral had transferred by means of the former vessel's cutter in the open sea, since it was impossible for the two to come alongside each other. Always a stickler for the correct formalities, particularly where these paid proper tribute to his rank, the redoubtable Ciliax, with his quaking staff in the rear, had descended the rope ladder hanging down the side of the first ship and, while the air above had been a frenzy of activity with aircraft and shellfire, climbed that to the new flagship, all to the accompaniment of the shrill calls of boatswains' pipes from the men on the quarterdecks.

But even this had happened well before midnight, and now it was a new day. Whether the cold that caused the crews to huddle deeper into their thick greatcoats on the wind-swept decks was due to a further deterioration in the temperature or whether it was the atmosphere of the more northerly port, it was difficult to say.

Among the many changes that marked the early hours of

Friday the 13th was the fact that now, despite the problems encountered with the field of mines, the *Gneisenau* had become the leading vessel and as such was the first to enter the familiar Heligoland Bight of the pre-war weather forecasts. The homecoming of the great vessel had not been without its problems and emergencies however, and even now there was a very real danger that she might be found by a British reconnaissance aircraft—a discovery which could alert the RAF bombers in a short time; one lucky, well-placed, armour-piercing bomb could mean her end. Alive to the possibility of defeat snatched from the mouth of success, Captain Fein on *Gneisenau*'s bridge eyed the lowering clouds and hoped that they would stay that way until the worst was over, for if they evaporated with the growing light, the additional aiming-height that their absence would give a bomber could result in just one carefully dropped missile going right through the armoured deck; if it exploded inside, it could still turn the proud battle-cruiser into a smoking hulk on the bottom, with only her superstructure showing— like that of *Graf Spee* that still rusted at the entrance to the harbour at Montevideo.

It almost seemed that the harbour authorities at Brunsbüttel had not expected the three capital ships to survive the voyage from Brest. If they did so, the traditional thoroughness of German temperament had failed on this occasion, for the first misfortune to be discovered at the homecoming was that there were no tugs available to tow the warship in; nor was there a pilot to be had. It wanted only the wail of the air-raid sirens to send their deep, hollow warning (quite unlike the higher-pitched British sound) to herald the coming of a force of aircraft like avenging angels from Hell to pound the ship that was now a sitting target.

In the circumstances, there were two possible courses of action. The ship could either drop anchor at the mouth of the River Elbe or steam up and down in the surface ice and wait for assistance. It was obvious that of the unattractive alternatives the former offered the slighter danger, for patrolling could well find another mine that would turn success into defeat.

The request for tugs and a pilot had not reached its destination up river, taken by a small ice-breaker in an attempt not to break radio silence, when the worst happened: the air-raid sirens began to howl into the freezing air. Soon after the anchor chain had rattled down the hawsepipes, the anti-aircraft gunners found themselves scanning the grey heavens from behind the shields of the weapons they had not been able to leave since the dramatic slide out of the French dock. If any remembered that their voyage had begun with a raid and bid fair to end with one, he kept it to himself and gave vent to his feelings only by blowing on his frozen hands the more frequently and stamping his feet more sharply on the frosty deck.

It was the sound of the warning-siren that seemed to help the captain to make up his mind, for by now the long-awaited tugs had appeared in the company of a small group of ice-breakers. It was still several hours before the maximum water would be under the keel of the great ship, but it was obviously the time to invoke 'Lady Luck' for the last time and try to get the battle-cruiser to sanctuary. As the engine-room telegraph rang down the call for the engines slow ahead, the wind, a cold south-wester, was beginning to rise, bringing flurries of snow as it did so.

Slowly, seemingly inch by painful inch, the grey-camouflaged bulk of the warship crept into the Brunsbüttel roadsteads with the officers on the bridge watching every movement of the straining tugs and the treacherous current. Then, in a moment, the waters seized the great vessel as if she had been a floating feather and swung her stern round almost in a half circle where the stone sides of the mole threatened to beat in the plates with one crushing blow. The thickly gloved hand on the handle of the telegraph swept it back across the dial to full speed astern, and as the crew below deck responded to the order, the moment of danger was passed. It was only for the shortest of breathing-spaces however, that those on the bridge could relax, for the backward movement in avoiding one disaster had created another: the drift of the aft swing was now taking the rear of the battle-cruiser full at a half-submerged wreck. With all attempts to avert this new disaster unavailing, the force of the tide took control of the situation and smashed the high stern against the wreckage with a metallic, booming crash that echoed into the frosty air. On the bridge an officer pushed back his cap in a reflex action to scratch his weary head as he thought of the date.

Once more the engine-room telegraph shrilled a demand for

the ship to go forward. For a moment it seemed as if she was inexorably fouled with the underwater trap, but slowly the *Gneisenau* responded to the urge of the motors and tore herself free, with the help of the now-freshened wind, but not before the ominous sound had once more ground into the early morning air to announce that the damage done had caused one of the propeller-tunnels to flood. So preoccupied were those on the bridge that few of them noticed that the sirens were again sounding, announcing that the danger from that direction had passed for the present at least; no raiders had appeared.

The warship was now in a potentially dangerous position. The extent of the damage could not be known, so it was deemed advisable to drop anchor and carry out an inspection while the tide rose and the engineers went about their work, knowing that full water was still more than an hour off. The tugs dropped the tow-lines and made their way out of sight up river.

It was something after 9 a.m. when the final report was made, to the effect that it was perfectly possible to proceed, but with caution, using only two propellers after the collision with the wreck. Since the tide was now at its height, it was decided to renew the attempt, and the tugs were again looked for to assist. Again there were none, and since any further delay would only bring fresh difficulties, the captain decided to carry on through the ice-capped water alone. Thus it was that KM *Gneisenau* came home to Germany. In the silence that followed the dropping of the anchor and cessation of the throb of the motors there was a pause before a new sound echoed through the vessel: weary as they were, for many had gone without sleep for twenty-four hours, the crew were cheering. They had achieved the seemingly impossible, and they knew it. For the moment at least all was right with the world.

Brunsbüttel lies at the western entrance to the Kiel Canal, and to reach it was in effect the mark of success for the officers and men of the Nazi squadron. With the alteration of the order of the vessels due to so many exigencies on the way, it was the *Prinz Eugen*, the cruiser which had been the last in the line, that was destined to reach haven next. Since the early part of the previous evening she had made slow progress, well to the inner limit of the prescribed course and at times so far beyond the vision of the look-outs on the marker-boats that they failed to spot her as she slipped along, sometimes as slowly as 7 knots, her grey upperworks making her seem almost part of the mist and gloom.

Dawn had not yet properly lit up the sky when the navigation officer was able to get a proper fix on their position, and thereafter the cruiser made better speed through the Bight where the *Hermann Schömann*, with Vice-Admiral Ciliax on board, was making good headway for the North Locks. Once more there was a fiasco with regard to tugs, and Captain Brinkmann had to make the same decision as his fellow officer on the battle-cruiser had before him. Like Fein, he realized that the position in which his charge was placed was a vulnerable one, so he too decided to sail up the estuary without aid.

The resultant journey was very much a repeat of the one made by the battle-cruiser, even to the trouble with the wreck that lay near to the entrance, but with this the *Prinz Eugen* fared rather better, and once it was passed, the journey through the ice was without event. Although the greater number of those on board the *Gneisenau* were hardly aware of the fact (snatching the first rest they had been able to take since France had receded into the night, as they left Brest some twenty-four hours before), the *Prinz Eugen* finally came to rest beside the larger vessel.

Off Wilhelmshaven lay a single marker-boat, and to the north of this had steamed the two capital ships. For *Scharnhorst*, limping after the emergency with the magnetic mine, the course at this point was to be slightly different, for Captain Hoffmann had now received orders from Admiral Ciliax to make direct to this port. Although the flotilla commander was well acquainted with her position, it seemed to those less well informed that the achievement might yet be a hollow one, for there was no news of the second battle-cruiser, and so orders were given that the fog-hooters were to sound a blast at two-minute intervals to give warning to the *Scharnhorst*, should she be in the vicinity.

In fact, at dawn she was very much in the area, although the mournful sounds blasted onto the bitter morning air did nothing to evoke an atmosphere of optimism in the minds of those who waited. Indeed, such was the certainty that the worst was over, while the first light was slashing patterns of light through the distant mists, that Otto Ciliax ordered the *Hermann Schömann* alongside a tug and from thence had transferred to the *Scharn-*

horst, where he took possession of his cabin.

By now the battle-cruiser was in the Weser estuary *en route* for the berth to which she had been directed at Wilhelmshaven south of the final marker-vessel. With the Admiral safely aboard, it seemed as if the troubles of *Scharnhorst* were all but over. This was not so. There were certainly two tugs now (the one bearing Otto Ciliax was the second on the scene), but still there was no pilot-boat, so an attempt to lead the battle-cruiser in was made by the skipper of one of the tugs. But both of these would have to drop their tow-lines before entering the sluice-gates before Wilhelmshaven, and after this obstacle was nego-tiated it was clear that she would receive as little help as the earlier ships had done. There was only one decision that Captain Hoffmann could make, and a moment later he announced that he was prepared to take his ship in without help.

The cold intense, and as the men on the bridge exchanged a few anxious words in the freezing morning air, their breath rose in clouds of steam into the still atmosphere. The feeling of winter's bitter grip was intensified by the thickness of the ice that covered the surface of the water—not enough to provide any major problem to navigation but sufficient to make the way slow. All the while the sound of the creaking and snapping of the frozen water in front of the bows filled the air as the ship crept along.

Having come so far and endured so much, the final phase of the journey was perhaps the most painful. All the time there was the risk of discovery and air attack, but nothing could be done about it, and some found the last painful progress almost as hard to bear as the period when *Scharnhorst* was hove to after the incident with the mine—an incident that the navigating officer, Giessler, had found particularly straining: he would tell about it for years after, adding that it was only the weather that had saved them from being found on that occasion and sent to the bottom as they floundered helplessly on the Channel swell.

With a painful slowness, the engine-room telegraph sounding its bells almost continuously, the great battle-cruiser made its way through the gates and on to its berth, the sound of the disintegrating ice all the time rising on the bitter air. As the last line was made fast and the throb of the engines died away, leaving in its stead a great silence that broke strangely on the ears long used to their note, the cheers that echoed forth were the signal that the operation had succeeded beyond the hopes of anyone concerned. Had only one of the great ships escaped from its prison at Brest, the desires of Hitler might have been satisfied; two would surely have vindicated the boldness of the plan; but to have the three come through was seemingly little short of the achievement of something impossible. True there was both damage and casualties, but nothing material had been done that could not be repaired.

Official recognition of the conclusion of the whole affair took the form of a signal sent to Paris by the Vice-Admiral, the cold formal words declaring: "It is my duty to inform you that 'Operation Cerberus' has been successfully completed. Lists of damage and casualties follow." Later, writing his full report, having received those of the captains in his cabin, the 'Black Czar' was to use a term that a few hours later was to be splashed across the front of almost every newspaper in Great Britain— not from the Nazi source but resorted to with unashamed readiness by Whitehall: "The weather . . . developed unfavourably for us . . . *and was advantageous to the enemy.*" But for just a short time longer the irony of the situation was to be hidden, for the four-page, frail newspapers that brought the first report of the whole sorry affair to the British breakfast-table that Friday morning said little more than was contained in the official communiqué under such headlines as "Scharnhorst in Great Channel Battle"—the full wrath was to come a little later.

Meanwhile the new bases of the three capital ships had suddenly become hives of activity. That it was only a matter of time, and probably but a short time, before the area should receive the same sort of punishment as Brest, was regarded as inevitable, but this apart there was still much to do of a more immediate nature.

Like their colleagues on the other vessels, all the crews wanted now was to rest and let sleep enfold their trammelled nerves, but Otto Ciliax was still the martinet he had always been, perhaps because of the stomach disorder that gave him no peace, so that work was in effect his only opiate. Just after 2 p.m. on the grey and freezing afternoon, the whistles rose once more into the dank air. This time they were piping all hands to the vast quarterdeck to hear an address by the Admiral. The serried ranks of more than eighteen hundred men listened under the augmented anti-aircraft guns to the words of exhortation with a polite silence that was almost sullen. At last they were dismissed to their duties, but only for a short while, for before dusk again descended to mark the end of the short winter day, they were summoned again, this time to hear Admiral Schniewind, Commander-in-Chief of the German Navy. It was with something akin to relief that the men completed their last duty—to hang the vessels with the thousands of square yards of camouflage-netting which had covered them so long in France.

In the small hours of the Friday morning it was obvious that the British 'Operation Fuller', the concerted plan to deny the English Channel to the Nazi warships, had not only failed but failed miserably, despite the determination of the men whose job it was to put into practical form the ideas of the planners—who might have experienced a fellow feeling with the Lancers at Balaclava and mused that it was "theirs not to reason why". However that may have been, there were many who would ask the same question on the Allied side and who are still doing so even at this distance in time.

First of these was obviously Winston Churchill, who had to be told of the grim situation. This unenviable task fell as his duty to the First Sea Lord, Sir Dudley Pound. This officer had led an eventful life and was then, by reason of his singular qualities, rightly the holder of the rank of admiral, but as he went to the telephone to state the dreadful truth to the Prime Minister, he was seen to square his shoulders. After he had told the worst, there was a silence at the other end of the telephone which seemed to last an age; then it was broken by the succinct voice which could distil eloquence into only a single word when the occasion demanded it; this was one such occasion and the monosyllable was all the more terrible for its brevity. "Why?" asked Churchill; without further ado the telephone went dead as the receiver was replaced at the other end.

It was just this question that was echoed in all the newspapers on the following Saturday in Britain. The editors had enjoyed sufficient time during the previous day to marshal their thoughts and arguments to ask in the most impassioned terms just the same thing. For once *The Times* dropped its traditional reserve and likened the event to the coming into the Channel of the Armada sent by Philip of Spain against the tiny Elizabethan Navy, but whereas the fleet of Admiral Medina Sidonia had received a thrashing, the modern enemy had escaped scot free.

Editors were, it seemed, at one in their condemnation of what had taken place. They seemed to go even beyond the bounds of solidarity that war and propaganda demanded. The Liberal *News Chronicle* which, like its fellows on the Saturday, now had what was seemingly the full story and which had had sufficient time to grasp the situation, declared in thick characters: "Air Spotters Sent Warning Too Late, says Navy," before going right to the heart of the matter with the question, "Where were the RAF reconnaissance planes that should have spotted the *Scharnhorst* and *Gneisenau* as, or immediately after, they left Brest?" The following remarks were those that almost echoed part of the report submitted to his superiors by Vice-Admiral Ciliax, when the writer went on in a tone of which the directness, unusual in wartime reporting, was ample illustration of the gravity of the situation: "The excuse that bad weather and visibility prevented adequate aerial reconnaissance is not accepted by the public here."

In similar vein the *Daily Mirror* took up the attack and presented the whole set of excuses with little comment, probably believing that they were sufficiently self-condemning. The reporter who asked, "Why was radio location [the contemporary name for radar] unable to locate warships and their umbrella of planes before Boulogne was reached?" and "Did the RAF make their usual inspection trips over Brest on Thursday morning?" was only pointing out the inadequacy of the official explanations which included such vague remarks as "The Germans chose their moment well . . . and we had only light forces."

But perhaps the last word from Fleet Street in the first flush of indignation was the almost Churchillian phraseology of 'Cassandra', who concluded his column that day with the dry observation that "Audacity still pays rich dividends." Something similar to that thought must have been in the mind of one of the least blameworthy officers in the whole dreadful business, Vice-Admiral Ramsay, when in a moment of cynicism he remarked that he was sure to be the official whipping-boy. As time was to tell, he was happily wrong in this particular.

In the rush to pacify public concern, certain authorities contradicted each other—an easy trap to fall into under the stress of war, when the propaganda value of the events which made up the news caused many agencies within the Services (who were not always in tune with the best traditions of the arms they spoke for) to make statements they must later have had cause to regret.

It therefore transpired that by the following Sunday the situation was becoming something of a muddle, and on the front page of one newspaper the serious matter of conflicting statements was given full billing with the headline: "Channel Battle Disclosure", but still there was the attempt to save face, with a blame on the weather, and the rider: "Vital weather from Dublin helped German battleships." However, the nub of the situation was then touched on with the next disclosure "Mystery of time-lag—fifty minutes between sighting and identification".

The cause of this claim had been the issue of twin statements, one from the RAF and the other from the Admiralty. The first had claimed that the enemy flotilla had been "spotted on Thursday morning" at 10.42 a.m. by "regular coastal patrols", while the second had contented itself with the surprising statement that the Nazi vessels had been "first identified" and reported at the entrance to the Straits of Dover at 11.35 p.m. Alert journalistic minds had immediately spotted just what these twin communiqués implied, and their questioning brought the next statement (which, for wartime, was dangerously near to an admission that the whole affair had been a muddle from start to finish) when the Admiralty spokesman said that, "There may have been an earlier report in nebulous terms, but the ships were not identified until 11.35 a.m."

The degree of disgrace felt by the public as a whole, mindful that Britain was a sea-going nation, was summed up well by Mr Hore Belisha MP, who was reported to have said that, "The passage of these three ships under the cliffs of Dover is the most significant event of the war." The degree to which it occupied the minds of persons at every level was shown by the call from Australia's Special Envoy, Sir Earle Page, who demanded that Britain learn "to think quicker; to act quicker". It was almost like rubbing salt into an open wound when, in a broadcast from Berlin Radio on the evening of the Saturday following the successful passage of the warships, Rear-Admiral Lutzow thundered: "This success is really shameful for the British Navy," before asking, "Once we have sailed from the Atlantic through the Channel to the North Sea, why should we not make the same journey in the opposite direction if it suits our plan?"

It must have seemed as if the rot of complacency had penetrated to the very heart of bureaucracy when it was reported in the British Press (from what it was claimed were official sources) that there would be no special enquiry, only a routine examination of the facts.

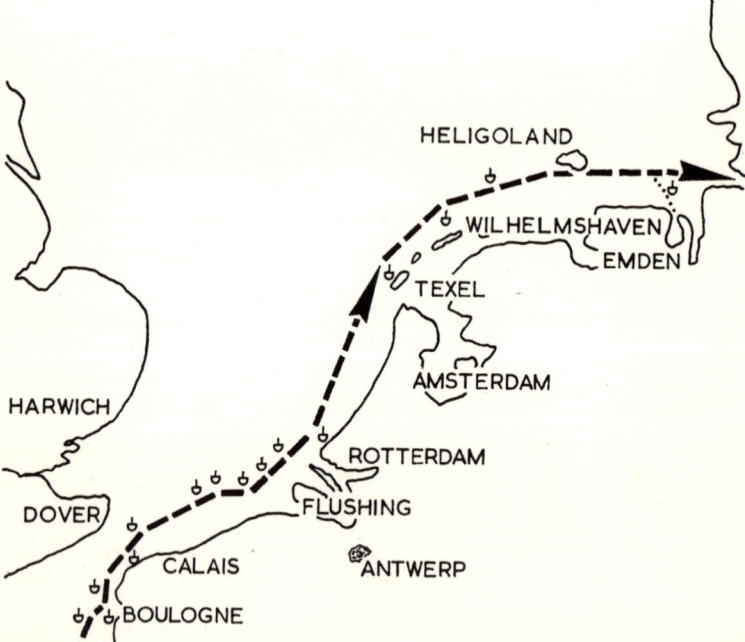

The course of the Nazi warships between Calais and Brunsbüttel

11

Court of Enquiry

Wherever the Sunday report that there would be no enquiry had come from, it was incorrect, for public indignation at the whole affair, whipped up by the newspapers to a higher pitch than might otherwise have been, had surprised even Churchill, who was by no means satisfied by any facet of the happenings on 12th February.

It was a case of justice not only being done but also being seen to be done, as far as the demands of a nation at war allowed. It was also done quickly for, moving with a speed unusual in bureaucratic circles, the Board to look into the matter was convened only four days after the event.

The scene could hardly have been better set for the last act of the drama, for the hearings were to be held not in some splendidly appointed room with thick carpet and immaculately polished horseshoe table but in an insignificant little cupboard of a room on the first floor of the Admiralty with slightly flaking buff-coloured walls similar to those found in barracks of the period and a small fire flickering in a Victorian iron gate.

It almost seemed that the weather had determined to make its contribution to the sombre scene, for as he hurried through the gloomy light of the morning of Monday 16th February, Mr Justice Bucknill, who was to preside, noted that the drizzle of the earlier hours had now set in determinedly.

To this day there survives a scrap of official note-paper, now yellowed and brittle so that the badge at the top is no longer clear, officially allocating the little room for the sorry hearing. It is called 'the Whitehall Room', and thousands still pass by on Horse Guards Parade and look up at its windows without realizing its place in history or even its existence.

As the hands of the Horse Guards clock moved to 11 a.m., the

Tribunal took their places behind a long plain table. To the right of the President sat Vice-Admiral Binney, and on the left of Mr Justice Bucknill was Air Chief Marshal Sir Edgar Ludlow-Hewitt, Inspector-General of the RAF, an officer who had less than two years before relinquished his post of Air Officer Commanding in Chief of Bomber Command after a three-year tour of duty.

While the first batch of witnesses waited, the President of the Tribunal formally read out the terms of reference. They were as simple as they were direct—namely that the circumstances of the passage of the Nazi capital ships be inquired into, and also the operations undertaken to intercept them. The signature at the bottom was the firm one that was now recognized and respected throughout not only Whitehall but also the greater part of the English-speaking world—the perimeters of investigation had been drawn up by Winston Churchill himself.

The witnesses who now waited for their turn to be called into the shabby inner room had time to examine their own thoughts. Some were bewildered; some were to welcome the chance of bringing to higher authority what they considered a national disgrace; others could not rid themselves of the feeling of surprise at the chain of events which had in less than a week found them out over the English Channel fighting to stay alive in a man-made Hell and then brought them to this situation on a cheerless Monday morning in a sand-bagged office in London. There was not far to search to discover the reasons for such a variety of reactions, for few of those who waited (they were of all ranks and conditions) were in any way professional fighting men, and the majority could conjure up in their minds the recollection of the recent past when they went daily to civilian jobs and worked in offices, shops and factories in a world that now seemed comfortable and cocooned, in days bounded at the one end by catching perhaps the crowded '8.21' and at the other by the evening paper, in which they had read of the latest goings-on of Hitler and British Prime Minister Chamberlain with a sort of vague detachment.

At this point in time there is nothing to be gained from the findings of the Board. The enquiry was certainly thorough within its terms of reference, but throughout the twelve days that it sat there was an unavoidable reluctance to accept that any great error had been made. This is not to say that the hearing was a 'whitewash operation', although there were cynics who claimed from first to last that it was, but rather that it is impossible for any group of men, however upright and honest they may be (and these qualities are unquestionable in the three on the tribunal convened), to divest themselves entirely if only in their personal sub-consciousness, from the atmosphere of the time. There is ample evidence that this state of affairs is just one of those frailties of human nature, and the early days of 1942 were the period in history when the manipulation of human thought (such as is now accepted to the point of maximum danger, namely that it is unrecognized) was passing from the stage where it was merely an imported gimmick employed by certain factions of the more popular Press to an exact science that was practised with government backing.

There were, however, particularly among the younger officers, those who, due to their closeness to the events and also their more alert minds were less ready to accept pre-digested opinions, those who spoke up frankly against what they saw as mismanagement in high places. The strength of their convictions was such that they were prepared to gamble on their Service careers to publicize them in the right places; they took risks for the sake of these convictions, for the opinions did not all go through the prescribed 'official channels'. It speaks well for the justice with which the findings of the Board were later studied that few, if any, significant moves were made against these courageous men—for they were no more than the spokesmen, in effect, for the larger part of the public who, although vocal, were unlikely to make use of the democratic processes, even though they were currently fighting for their preservation, to make their feelings known.

It was not until the war was over that Command Paper 6775, otherwise the Bucknill Report, was tabled in the form of a government White Paper in 1946. (This is hardly surprising.) However, it was ready for Parliament on 18th March, when Mr Clement Attlee as Deputy Prime Minister told the House that, "The general feelings do not reveal that there were any serious deficiencies either in foresight, co-operation or organization." In the exigencies of war he could voice no other opinion, but no one was satisfied. Admiral of the Fleet Lord Chatsfield, opening a county Warship Week for the National Savings Movement, was speaking for more than he probably knew when he declared that "Co-operation between the services is necessary", adding that, "Unfortunately we started the war with a navy that was too small and seventy-five per cent too old." The wisdom of this remark was unfortunately largely lost until now, for it laid the blame on a group of persons who were to escape the wrath of the Bucknill tribunal, the planners and advocates of soft complacency of the days before the Munich Crisis. The time was lost when measures could have been introduced with comparative economy—measures which would have made any potential aggressor have a moment of hesitation; they were only resorted to after the proverbial eleventh hour had gone. These men, or at least their successors, are still with us, ignorant of the harm they do in the role of the 'enemy' within as their parsimony saps morale.

In 1942 the Bucknill Report was concerned with more immediate guilt. One of its findings came down with severity on No 11 Group of Fighter Command which, in its view, was "not sufficiently alive" to the likely emergence of the Nazi warships —a surprising statement for, as we have seen, Coastal Command's AOC-in-C, Sir Philip Joubert, had made clear his fears of just such a course of events at an earlier date, even going so far as to predict a likely date.

To this must be added another facet touched on in the same paragraph of the findings, namely that some of the witnesses were not informed that the link that was provided by the airborne surveillance (by such as the 'Stopper' and 'Hobo' patrols) was temporarily broken, so that, the human animal being a lazy creature, there had been seemingly no call to look into the first reporting of the Nazi ships with any increased depth, nor to view the widening picture with any suspicion. It was a classic illustration of the way in which an excessive and unjustified zeal, even to the point of foolishness (for secrecy even existed between representatives of the same Command), had in fact been of paramount assistance to the enemy. There were, among those who had knowledge of the Board's findings, some who had heard Churchill conclude a statement to the House with an assurance that he was anxious to make it clear that matters were not "conducted by simpletons and dunderheads"—they must have remembered and wondered.

In general, however, the implied criticisms were of a fairly mild nature, and the probable reasons for this have already been made clear, but it seems that, despite their cautious nature, the findings were not lost on authority. Retribution (for this is what it was in the eyes of the public eagerly seeking a scapegoat) was not long in coming, although all was carried out in the most discreet and British way when it was suddenly announced that the two principal actors in the tragic enactment in the Channel were about to be elevated to new postings—'kicked upstairs' as Service parlance would term it.

The two were the C-in-C of Coastal Command and Fighter Command's 11 Group Commander, Sir Trafford Leigh-Mallory. Sir Philip's removal to a posting where little harm could be done was as unexpected as it was, some said, unjust, but it was only too easy to read into the findings of the tribunal a greater criticism of these two officers' conduct than was at first seemingly stated. However that may be, there are casualties in war, and not all of them are physical hurts brought about with high explosive. This has always been the case, and there are several examples to be found in wars of the present century. These were of a fairly mild and indeed militarily justified nature. The advent of civilian involvement in modern conflict with the removal of the fighting from the distant responsibility of the trained warrior, has meant that the new combatant, the unwilling civilian who must now carry the consequences for the ultimate blunderings of the politician as much as the fighting man, demands that his own form of justice be seen to be done, although this is often rough and based on an incomplete understanding of the situation so that it is first cousin to lynch law. The removal of Air Chief Marshal Sir Philip Joubert de la Ferté to a harmless post was therefore not entirely justified—unless one views the matter in the light of the belief that the officer must take responsibility for the actions of his subordinates, whether they are success or failure. Be that as it may, the former C-in-C of Coastal Command soon found himself repaid for his warnings and accurate analysis of the Nazi attempt by being posted to the staff of Lord Louis Mountbatten in Ceylon, with responsibility for the Direction of Information and Civil Affairs, a task having only the slightest connection with aviation and none at all with operations against the enemy. In this way public confidence in Service officers was not shaken, while the thirst for someone's 'blood' was also appeased.

With regard to Sir Trafford Leigh-Mallory, the situation is more complex—no doubt because he posed a more difficult problem with which to deal. Like Sir Philip, he was one of the 'old school' of senior officers who found it difficult to associate himself with the ordinary fighting man—which he had been himself twenty-four years before (the time between had been taken up largely with command of the Imperial Defence College, the School of Army Co-operation, instructional work and staff duties). Added to this was the fact that he found it difficult to establish any form of popularity, and some went so far as to call him pompous, an epithet which seems to be borne out by his preoccupation with respect due to his rank. That this Air Marshal was ambitious, there is no question. There is no great harm in the quality, particularly if it ensures that a man does his best in his responsibilities, but in this case ambition went hand in hand with a certain forceful nature, which meant not only that a number of colleagues had been collected of a similar temperament but also that the problem of what to do in the matter of the Channel escape was exacerbated.

The first time Sir Trafford had really come into the public eye was during the period less than two years before when he had been in command of No 12 Group of Fighter Command during the Battle of Britain. It was then that the theory of the 'big wings' was evolved, the idea that the best method of countering the Nazi Luftwaffe lay in the formation of large groups of interceptors made up of whole squadrons, and that various combinations of these could result in wings consisting of perhaps three or as many as seven squadrons in the air at one time. This tactic was in its way excellent, for it meant that huge slaughter could be done among the invading bombers, but the price to pay for this advantage was that the time taken to form up such a large number of fighters was frequently excessive, and therefore quite often the actual interception could be carried out only after the bombers had dropped their loads and were returning to base. The theory of the 'big wing' was therefore workable only in the area over which Sir Trafford had control, namely No 12 Group, since this was situated sufficiently far from the immediate emergencies of the south and south-east coasts, so that there was a longer warning-time in which to amass the fighters.

That adherence to this theory led to friction between the Group-Commander and his opposite number in the area on 12 Group's southern flank is now part of history, and it is quite obvious that the multiple-squadron tactic was not at the time operationally feasible in No 11 Group under the conditions in which it had to fight at that time.

Examination of the measure of which Sir Trafford was the architect and exponent has been here examined at some length because it tends to show quite clearly the characteristics of this officer and his outlook.

By the time of the break-out from Brest of the *Scharnhorst*, *Gneisenau* and *Prinz Eugen*, Trafford Leigh-Mallory had succeeded the brilliant Sir Keith Park in command of 11 Group and was consequently in command of the fighter cover over the Channel through which the Nazi vessels were to pass. It is only necessary to look at the situation quite briefly to form the opinion that in the theory of the multiple-squadron tactics lay the whole of Sir Trafford's policies. Indeed, at a later period of the conflict the adoption of these methods was certainly justified and paid dividends, but that was during the later times when the broader tactical behaviour of the Luftwaffe could be anticipated with a fair degree of accuracy.

Leigh-Mallory's particular tactical ability plainly lay in the direction of meticulous pre-planning. This was not surprising in a man of somewhat inflexible views, for the possession of this characteristic would naturally place him at a disadvantage when dealing with the cut and thrust of hour-to-hour emergency, unless, that is, the whole was on a broader, more foreseeable pattern.

There may be some who would, even in the light of this clear evidence, submit that none of it would appear to justify the claim that Sir Trafford merited to be dealt with in as severe a manner as his brother officer in Coastal Command. At first sight this would appear to be true, but a moment's reflection does leave the impression that a certain responsibility was read into the findings of the Bucknill Report. Thus the 'kick upstairs', although not perhaps administered with a booted foot, was still

there, even if administered by a foot in a sock sufficiently thick
not to damage public confidence. In his elevation to AOC-in-C
of Fighter Command, no less, Leigh-Mallory was re-mustered
into a post where his qualities as a tactician and academic
planner were put to their greatest advantage. At the same time
the posting removed him finally from a position of immediate
operational command with effect from December of the year of
the Channel fiasco. There he was to distinguish himself in the
preparation for 'Operation Overlord', the Allied invasion of the
continent of Europe that was still more than two years distant,
by developing an almost impregnable Fighter Command. He
was at last a square peg in a hole of the same shape. Appointed in
later years to command the Allied Air Forces in South-East
Asia, Air Chief Marshal Sir Trafford Leigh-Mallory, KCB, CB,
DSO, was making the journey to take up his new post in
company with his wife when both were killed on 14th November 1944, when the aircraft in which they were flying crashed
at Grenoble.

The reason 'why', as posed in Winston Churchill's cryptic
question is not so simply disposed of, for there were other issues
to be looked into, which went far beyond the condemnation of
individuals or even groups. One of these was the state of preparedness of Coastal Command and to a lesser extent of their
Bomber Command counterparts.

In looking at these one must remember, as the tribunal in the
Admiralty room in sight of Horse Guards Parade undoubtedly
did, that the entire thinking that coloured the whole of the
preparations for the interception of the ships by 'Operation
Fuller' was that the dash up the English Channel would be
carried out under cover of darkness. As we have seen earlier,
there was a minority who would disagree with this, but being a
minority their views were not seriously examined. One wonders
if Hitler's judgement of the situation as he sat among his officers
at 'Wolfsschanze' was in fact more accurate than we care to
admit, even at this distance in time. An island race is all too
often hidebound, a characteristic that is only partly balanced by
their arrogance in battle. The fact that there was a shrewd
judgement of British temperament is shown by the lack of
inter-service co-operation throughout the period and one that
the Bucknill Report seems to have chosen for viewing with a

Nelsonian blind eye, although its existence was made abundantly clear in the several private reports that were submitted and was also only too obvious in the recollections that were noted from the several interviews.

In its dealing with the reaction of the two main aerial strike forces, there is much to confirm that they were at a disadvantage, although this was a handicap that was much of their own making. Perhaps the one most readily appreciated is the position of the bombers (remembering that all the strikes from this part of the RAF took place after lunch-time and many towards the end of the day) for the slow reaction was due entirely to the fact that the structure and organization of the Command was based on the concept that a target was not mobile and that there would be, if not ample, certainly adequate time to make preparation, so that, suddenly alerted, the whole process was incapable of meeting the demands made on it—a very dangerous precept for any fighting service and one which modern tactical thinking is, not always with complete success, only now attempting to eliminate.

With regard to Coastal Command it should not be overlooked that, although the presence of the three ships in Brest was keeping a large part of British resources tied down in this corner of western Europe, it was commonly regarded at the time that the next focal-point of the war would be outside the European theatre. Therefore the standards of delivering a swift and conclusive strike by torpedo aircraft had been allowed to lapse so that the greater weight of responsibility fell on the gallant crews of the six elderly Swordfish biplanes which were themselves only semi-trained for what was in effect a one-way suicide mission.

Throughout all this sorry parade of misguided effort, inefficiency, personal axe-grinding and some plain bad luck, there is a marked absence of any naval contribution on the grand scale, an unexpected omission in a country that prided itself (one hopes still does) on being a maritime nation for which the navy was a "sure and certain shield". Here again there is the unfortunate appearance of an individual name, and is that of the First Sea Lord at the time, Admiral Sir Dudley Pound. To mention it in connection with the case is all the more sorry since the Admiral had given of his best for many years and had proved

himself very much suited for the duties he discharged as First
Sea Lord. Nevertheless he suffered from one serious precon-
ception, and this was the vulnerability of his capital ships if
directed to operations in the coastal waters that the Nazi squadron must use if an escape was attempted. It therefore turned out
that the work of surface interception was left entirely to the
MTBs and MGBs with the additional backing of the ageing
destroyers. There never could be another Battle of Jutland
involving Nazi versus British capital ships, it was decided, and
this fact must be viewed for the sake of accuracy from the
viewpoint that there was an equal chance that the enemy flotilla
might make a dash for Atlantic waters as much as for the haven
of a German port.

The reasons stated therefore for the lack of battleships which
might have countered the break-out is that to order them south
would have possibly placed them in danger of minefields and of
air attack, although the successful conclusion of 'Operation
Cerberus' by the German Navy must in the final analysis have
posed several questions as to just how vulnerable capital ships
could be to ferocious attention from the air.

However, an Admiralty statement revealed that, of the three
ships available, one, *Rodney*, was waiting to be refitted, and of
the other two, *Renown* was stated to be actively engaged in
providing cover for a convoy for the Middle East, and *King
George V* was covering a possible departure from Trondheim of
Tirpitz, which was at the same moment in time emulating, so to
speak, the other three capital ships in France.

It is certainly a known fact that the AOC-in-C of Coastal
Command did make strenuous efforts to secure the presence of
one or other of these vessels near the south coast. But on each
occasion he was frustrated by the determination of the First Sea
Lord to have none of it, despite the fact that the risk taken in the
nature of a calculated one since, temporarily based at a port on
the east cost, the *King George V*, for example, could have
provided cover during the period of maximum danger.

12

Hindsight

On 12th February 1982 the whole business of the flight of the two Nazi battle-cruisers and the heavy cruiser up the English Channel will have been over and done with for forty years and will be thus no more than an event in the history books, a story with which the ageing bore the young. The survivors may pause and look at themselves with surprise, not only that they have been spared to reminisce but that the impossible has happened: the process which only seemed to overtake other people has themselves in its grip—time has stolen their youth. All that had seemed so important and vital has vanished, and the world has fulfilled none of their hopes but has spun time remorselessly away. A new set of vital tenets has evolved for their children. Now the great battle is as much history as Trafalgar or the fireships at Cadiz, and only schoolmasters and historians seem to care. The compilers of human record say it was a Nazi victory; apart from that, it is sterile, past and dry, another date in the record of man's folly.

Yet, how true is the claim of defeat on that cold and mist-shrouded February morning? Churchill saw the position more clear-sightedly than most when he pointed out that the removal of the ships from the harbour at Brest where they had lain for so long had made a real contribution to the flexibility of the British war-effort, for the large number of aircraft that their presence called for to carry out the long-drawn-out series of attacks could now be released for use in the wider theatre of operations. True, although he claimed this at the time, and it was not, as a few believed, mere propaganda, it was still necessary to order the Board of Enquiry, for although there was certainly an element of success for the Allies in Hitler's seemingly rash demand that the Operation be attempted at all costs it was still vital that the fears and alarms felt by the public be laid and that the gross inefficiency of the attempts to put 'Fuller' into motion be rooted out. In practical terms, although the Nazis had achieved a tactical success, they had done so by making a strategic withdrawal, and it was carried out from the very bases that had seemed on the occupation of France to offer such inviting prospects for the furtherance of the war at sea. It was the end of the offensive in the Atlantic as it had originally been planned.

Nevertheless, there remained the struggle to convince the public of the value that lay within the muddle which had received so much publicity. Also something in the way of reassurance was called for on a personal level within the Services, a fact that applied equally on both sides, although those made to the Nazi seamen were meagre. For his part in commanding the whole operation, the Knight's Cross was awarded to Vice-Admiral Ciliax—fittingly, for this was one of the highest decorations possible, being reserved for holders of either the First or Second Class Iron Cross; the same went to Kurt Hoffmann of the *Scharnhorst*. Otto Fein of *Gneisenau* went undecorated, as did Captain Brinkmann of the *Prinz Eugen*.

The British were more generous, although there have been those who have attempted to tarnish for their own ends the validity of the awards by implication that they were bestowed as a sort of act of contrition after the dreadful revelations of inefficiency that the day had brought to light. There is little evidence, if any, that this was the case.

Fittingly, the supreme award for gallantry was made posthumously to Lieutenant-Commander Eugene Esmonde who, the *London Gazette* was to announce, had been given the Victoria Cross for which he had been recommended in the report penned in the awareness of the moment by the Manston station-commander. Eugene's mother received the Cross from the hands of King George VI at Buckingham Palace on 17th March —a gesture suggested by the King since it was St Patrick's Day.

To be present, Mrs Esmonde had to display something of the grit and determination that had distinguished the family for hundreds of years, since, stricken with arthritis as she was, movement without the aid of a wheelchair was an ordeal. At first it seemed that the width of the Irish Sea was to form a barrier that could not be spanned, but her surviving sons had other ideas. (Four of them were already serving in the British armed forces: Patrick, in the Royal Army Medical Corps, Witham in the Royal Navy, and Owen in the RAF, with Donal in Holy Orders.) The solution to the problem of how to bring Mrs Esmonde from her home in Tipperary, in neutral Ireland, to London was solved when the de Havilland Dominie plane normally reserved as an 'admiral's barge' by the Fifth Sea Lord was placed at her disposal. The worries seemed to be over, but this was by no means the case, for when the machine was on the way from Scotland, the weather began to close in, and while it was on course over the Irish Sea the weather worsened, so that an emergency landing had to be made on the Isle of Man. After a wait of about an hour, it seemed as if the climate relented, for conditions improved sufficiently for the biplane to become airborne once more. All seemed to be going according to plan when the radio crackled into life and a metallic voice over the pilot's headphones informed the flyers that they were heading straight for an air raid that was at the very moment being made on Belfast. This was not all, for the city was defended by a balloon barrage. To avoid these hazards the voice diverted the machine to land at a different aerodrome some distance away.

Even after Mrs Esmonde had been collected, it seemed that the weather was determined to ruin matters, but despite this the machine to which the mother and son (Patrick of the Medical Corps was acting as courier) were rushed by special car was in the air once again the following afternoon.

At about 10 a.m. the next day, Mrs Esmonde found herself at the gates of Buckingham Palace. Her progress was slow, despite the assistance of Patrick and now Owen, who had joined them, for the wheelchair had been too large to be loaded through the door of the aircraft and had been left behind. Until now this had not been too serious a problem, for another car had been provided, again by courtesy of the Fifth Sea Lord, to take the Esmondes from Hendon, where the de Havilland machine had landed, to the hotel where they had spent the night. Then, in a flash, all the problems vanished: from somewhere a sergeant produced a wheelchair, and it was from this that the lady received the Victoria Cross on behalf of her dead son who had stood on the same spot to receive the DSO from the King only a short time before the three warships in France had broken from their prison at the start of a chain of events that was to end in his death. As the same aircraft returned Mrs Esmonde to her home, it seemed as if the King's wishes were being fulfilled, for the weather was unusually clear and sunny for the time of year.

This was not all, for there is a poignant footnote to the little ceremony at Buckingham Palace. It had been assumed that the earthly remains of Eugene Esmonde had found a sailor's tomb in the English Channel, but about a month later a dark shape bobbing on the surface of the Thames Estuary proved to be the body of a man in the uniform of an officer of the Royal Navy and the gold wings proved that he was a flyer. When the body was tossed ashore on the Kent coast, it at once became clear that the reason for the corpse being carried along with the tide was that it was supported in the water by a partly inflated life-jacket. An ambulance was called, and the body of the man was removed so that closer examination might be possible before it was prepared for burial. It was then that the body was discovered to be that of Lieutenant-Commander Eugene Esmonde who had led the hopeless attack by the half-dozen Swordfish biplanes against the three capital ships.

All the survivors of this doomed band were to receive awards. The four Sub-Lieutenants were given the Distinguished Service Order, and Donald Bunce, the gunner, who was the only rating to live, was awarded the Conspicuous Gallantry Medal.

There were naval decorations for Captain C. T. M. (later Admiral Sir Mark) Pizey, who had led the Harwich destroyer force and who became a Commander of the Bath, and for Captain Wright DSO of *Mackay*, who received a bar to that decoration. Colin Coates of the much-punished *Worcester* was given the Distinguished Service Order, as were *Whitshed*'s Lieutenant-Commander Juniper and W. A. Juniper of HMS *Whitshed*. The RAF likewise decorated its heroes, many of the awards going to Coastal Command, although the horror of the day is fittingly shown by the fact that, of the total number of awards made, no less than fourteen were posthumous.

Hardly had the action receded into the recent past than the historians got to work. The tale that they uncovered was no less dreadful than the findings of the Bucknill tribunal and the way seemed strewn with tales of failure interspersed with gallantry on both sides. The degree of ineptitude that so marked the day is brought sharply home by the discovery that the minefield through the terrors of which Lieutenant-Commander Coates thought he was painfully guiding his battered *Worcester* had no substance, for it had been earlier cleared; the fact had not been released to ships' captains; Coates's painful creeping passage was in vain.

But there are other facts that should be recorded in order that the saga of the fateful February day may be complete, and in this last act the principal players are once more the three Nazi ships whose escape began the chain of events.

In their new locations the two battle-cruisers and the cruiser were still within range of the Royal Air Force, although now their distance placed them entirely within the scope of Bomber Command. The fact that this was known only too well to the enemy was shown by the anxious time that the crews spent waiting for the non-existent tugs while they scanned the skies for the avenging angels that all knew must come. In fact almost the last voyage of the three had already taken place.

A fortnight after the audacious passage up the Channel the air-raid warnings wailed over the docks at Kiel. The encounter with the mine had meant that the inspection which followed the arrival of the *Gneisenau* and her sister ship there had called for the transfer of the former into dry dock. The date was 25th February.

With the anti-aircraft guns hurling a curtain of death into the sky, the first wave of bombers came in to the attack, flying as if they had been performing at a royal review. It seemed as if nothing could stop their inexorable passage through the winter sky. With deadly precision the first dropped their loads, which sent up a fountain of fire and smoke from the centre of the dock area. Then came the second wave, as undeterred by the artillery as the first. These were succeeded by further formations, each bent on the end of the ships below as still the bombers swept over, until a total of over sixty had passed.

With the morning light came the job of clearing up, but hardly had this been completed than, with the following darkness, the sirens made the night hideous once more with their eerie howls. The pause between the first warning and the onset of gunfire (above which could be heard the sound of engines) only seemed to make the waiting longer. Then it came—a gradual swelling of the beat of the motors and the roar of the guns until the night was filled with the noise of battle. At intervals there rolled across the dock complex the roar of the exploding bombs. The aiming of the bombers was accurate and deadly. Few of the missiles fell outside the area, and it seemed that a determined effort was being made by the force (which was smaller than that of the night before but still amounting to almost fifty in number) to pound the battle-cruiser where she lay under the camouflage-netting in the waterless dock.

She was not alone in her suffering, for a short distance away, at Wilhelmshaven, the *Scharnhorst* was at the receiving-end of a smaller visitation from Bomber Command. There were only just over thirty machines, but they were as seemingly deadly as the others which continued to make the darkness a Hell as the searchlights probed and the crump of the explosions marched across the dock area until it seemed impossible that a bomb could not pierce the thick armoured deck and explode inside the great hull.

With the first streaks of light breaking across the sky to the east, a great silence had fallen on the area after the sound and fury of the night, broken now only by the rising note of the 'raiders past' siren. The dawn broke on a scene of desolation in the centre of which lay the bulk of the *Gneisenau* with a great hole blasted in her bows where an armour-piercing bomb had struck. The sixty-eight bombers had done their work well.

In the months that followed, the fate of the battle-cruiser seemed symptomatic of the attitude which was developing, to the effect that the day of the big warship was nearly over; yet there were those who could still champion their cause.

Still the devastating raids went on, whenever the weather offered a chance. Typical of the smaller attacks was that carried out on the night of 4th September when fourteen Wellingtons dropped bombs on both of the battle-cruisers. Although on that occasion neither was hit, although two bombers were lost.

At about this time, in preparation for the fitting of 15-inch guns, those of 11-inch calibre were removed with their turrets, two being added to the coast defences of Norway and another being set up in Holland. But the writing was on the wall for the older order of fighting ship, and the matter came to a head in 1943 when the *Gneisenau, Tirpitz, Scharnhorst, Lützow, Admiral*

Hipper and *Prinz Eugen* were all scheduled for scrapping—although in the event a temporary reprieve was granted for some. However, Hitler was now preoccupied with manpower and material shortages, and refits already begun were immediately abandoned. In March of the following year the hulk of the *Gneisenau* made its last voyage, under tow to Gydnia on Poland's Baltic Coast where she was filled with concrete and scuttled to act as a blockship; it was not until after the war in September 1951 that the remains were finally removed and broken up by the Soviet Navy.

Her sister ship, the *Scharnhorst*, lasted a little longer on the active list, being the subject of a plan issued on February 1943 that she would be temporarily kept in service for a further three months with the *Prinz Eugen* in Baltic waters. Then she was to be relegated to training-duties with the emphasis on seamanship instruction for U-boat crews, although it was anticipated at the time that the battle-cruiser might well prove surplus for this work, and if this was the case, it was proposed that she be broken up at the end of the summer.

September 1943 found the *Scharnhorst* the subject of a lucky escape when, during the night of the 22nd, Lang Fjord, a branch of Alten Fjord where she lay with the *Tirpitz*, was pierced by four midget submarines, despite the anti-torpedo booms and submarine nets. Two of the British vessels succeeded in planting special mines beneath the *Tirpitz* which did sufficient damage to immobilize her for six months, but despite the proximity of the two vessels, *Scharnhorst* remained unscathed.

From this haven the battle-cruiser emerged only once between 6th and 9th September when, with the battleship, she formed part of a force that included nine destroyers sent in a raid on Spitzbergen. Her next trip into the open sea was not to take place until the night of 25th-26th December the same year, when she quit the fjord with a task force of destroyers in a south-westerly gale; the flotilla steamed rapidly towards the twin prizes offered by convoys to and from Russia, JW55B outward bound with an escort of two corvettes, a frigate and fourteen destroyers, and RA55A heading home under the protection of ten warships, six destroyers and four corvettes. All these movements were known to the Admiralty in London, which at 3.30 a.m. had signalled Admiral Fraser, the C-in-C, Home Fleet, on board the *Duke of York* details of the enemy's movements, even the intelligence that the battle-cruiser had later failed to keep contact with the destroyers and was, according to plan, proceeding alone.

The situation was one for which the British Admiral had prepared for some time, and two units were engaged. The first, designated Force 1, consisted of HMS *Belfast*, with Vice-Admiral Burdett aboard, *Norfolk* and *Sheffield*. Force 2 was made up of the C-in-C's *Duke of York*, *Jamaica* and four destroyers from the Royal Norwegian Navy, *Savage*, *Scorpion*, *Stord* and *Saumarez*. Since it was unlikely that the second of these units could reach the area in time, the outward convoy was ordered to reverse its course for three hours while Force 1 shadowed it to see that it came to no harm from *Scharnhorst*.

It was 8.40 a.m. when the radar in *Belfast*'s operations room first began to register the presence of the Nazi vessel. Just before 9.30 p.m. fire was opened with starshells in what was to be the Battle of North Cape. *Norfolk* fired a broadside, the second or third salvo of which hit the port bridge director severely while another struck the forecastle with lesser effect.

However, although the three cruisers were now able to shadow the retreat of *Scharnhorst*, the range increased as her speed was superior by 6 knots, and the Nazi set a north-east course which would bring her into range of the convoy. Thus the cruisers altered course to place themselves between the two, and *Belfast* later re-established radar contact. Fire was once more exchanged, during which *Norfolk* sustained some hits at 11,000 yards, but the subsequent course of the enemy indicated that hopes of attacking the convoy had been abandoned.

With the time approaching 5 p.m., both *Belfast* and the elements of the second force were in range, the *Duke of York* firing her 14-inch guns at about 6 miles range while *Belfast* again opened with starshells as the battle was being carried on in complete darkness some 500 miles inside the Arctic Circle.

Meanwhile the British second force was being shadowed from the coast of Norway by a Blom und Voss 138 flying-boat. Communication with the battle-cruiser was impossible as there was no direct radio link since the ship operated on a different channel, but the enemy seemed oblivious of the presence of

Duke of York and *Jamaica*, despite their being in view of the aircraft. The tactics of the Nazi were to make a southward turn to fire a broadside and immediately present a smaller target with an eastern turn until ready to engage again, so that the gunners in the *Duke of York* experienced difficulties until similar measures were taken by the British ships to give the destroyers a chance to move in undetected. In the exchange of fire that followed, 'A' turret was put out of action by the *Duke of York*, and the *Scharnhorst's* 'C' turret was damaged, but the engagement was broken off as the range opened to 21,400 yards.

The destroyers had closed to 7,000 yards when they came under heavy but none too accurate fire, but they closed to a minimum of 1,800 yards to send in their torpedoes. Hits were made, one of them in the battle-cruiser's boiler-room. Although *Saumarez* suffered damage and casualties as a result, her speed was reduced to only 10 knots.

Force 2 meanwhile closed the range, and the enemy suffered further hits, while at much the same time the Nazi destroyers had begun a search for the *Scharnhorst* over the assumed course to the south-west. There was now a heavy sea running, and the crews found difficulty in standing upright. A snowstorm began, and in the midst of this a heavy explosion was heard from the direction of the battle-cruiser. Worse was to follow, for a little later shells struck home "from nowhere", and the 'Seetakt' radar (which the enemy had failed to use for fear of giving their position away) was damaged when the shells wrecked the fore-tops. The fire was returned, but ranging was only on the muzzle-flashes, which must have indicated that the target was *Norfolk*, as the others were using a new flashless powder. A severe hit was obtained forward and another aft, and a third put one of the turrets out of action. *Musketeer*, *Matchless*, *Opportune* and *Virago* now swept in, and further hits were claimed on the battle-cruiser.

Exactly when *Scharnhorst's* end came is still a subject for conjecture. *Jamaica* closed in to 2 miles range and opened fire on a target that had been slowed by the *Duke of York's* 14-inch guns. Shortly afterwards a dull red glow was seen suddenly through the fog. She capsized bow first, with the great stern rearing up, the propellers still turning. For *Scharnhorst* 'Operation Ostfront' was over. Only thirty-six men were rescued from the freezing water. No officers survived.

Destined to last longest of the three ships that had passed up the Channel in February 1942 was the *Prinz Eugen*. In the summer of 1944 she was directed with the *Lützow* and *Admiral Scheer* to act as additional artillery in support of the rearguard action being carried out by the Army, with naval action directed by Vice-Admiral August Thiele. But even in this the *Prinz* seemed dogged by ill luck, for, in common with the remainder of the force, frequent withdrawals were necessary for a change of gun-barrels and replenishment of ammunition and fuel. Thus it was that the cruiser survived to be surrendered intact on 25th May 1945 at Copenhagen. From there she journeyed to Boston, Massachusetts, *en route* for Bikini Atoll for the United States atomic-bomb tests in 1946. The wreck that the nuclear explosion left was towed out to sea and scuttled at Kwajalein a year later.

The British warships too survived the war but were to pass quickly from the scene. The first to go was HMS *Walpole*, scrapped at Grays in March 1945, followed by the redoubtable *Worcester* re-named *Yeoman* in 1945 only to be sold to the breakers on 17th September a year later. February 1947 saw the scrapping of *Whitshed*, *Campbell* and *Mackay*, leaving the final survivor, and the oldest, *Vivacious*, which had been commissioned in mid-November 1917, to be rendered into scrap at Charlestown in October 1948.

Thus ended one of the best-remembered and most unhappy events of the Second World War. The Nazis had finally called it 'Operation Cerberus'; the British precautions were coded 'Fuller'; but the provision of air support for the Channel dash had been called 'Operation Thunderbolt' by the Nazi Luftwaffe. The choice of name was most fitting; it was far more prophetic than could have ever been imagined at the time, and its explosion on the British complacence, for which the pattern had been established by the guilty men of the 1930s, did more than anything else to alert public and Service awareness that the price of peace is eternal vigilance. This time the realization had been too dearly bought—a thunderbolt indeed.

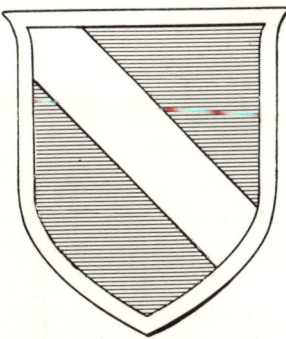 

Above: The badges carried in full colour on the bows of (left) Scharnhorst and (right) Gneisenau. The arms below were associated with the Prinz Eugen, formerly a traditional name in the Austro-Hungarian Navy, as that of Prince Eugène of Savoy, the Habsburg Lieutenant-General of the eighteenth-century Holy Roman Empire and co-commander, with Marlborough, in the War of Spanish Succession. The arms were carried by the vessel only in the form of a placard at the launching ceremony and were not permanently borne as were the others.

The badges of *Scharnhorst*, *Gneisenau* and *Prinz Eugen*

Epilogue

"OK Sir?"

"OK Jess!" With the ritual slap of the hand on the fuselage of the Spitfire, a Mark V, numbered W3649 with the prominent letters FV B on the side, Sergeant Jessop slid off the wing. There was no need for a greatcoat now for it was the end of March, and the Saturday brought a promise of spring to the air at Kenley as the NCO turned to watch the Station-Commander take off.

The previous days had been full of activity, a period ushered in on the afternoon of Friday the 27th when Group-Captain Beamish had led a formation to cover a bombing-sortie over Le Havre. He had just sent a Messerschmitt 109 down and had watched it explode before hitting the ground when the voice of his Wing-Commander crackled over the radio, alerting him to another enemy fighter on the Spitfire's tail. With the reflex action of the experienced air fighter, Victor Beamish flung the nose of his machine sharply up to miss the French cliffs by a distance that he was later to describe as "a bit too close for my liking". He turned on his pursuer, pressed on the rudder-bar to bring it into his sights and squeezed the teat on his control-grip. A short burst was enough, and the Messerschmitt plummeted into the cliffs that had so recently almost claimed himself.

On the journey back, it was fighting all the way, and one of the pilots had to bale out. There were plenty of others who could have been detailed to cover the man now bobbing about in the Channel until a rescue launch arrived, but this was not the Group-Captain's way: he swung off from the formation to do the job himself.

The following afternoon provided weather conditions that were ideal for an offensive sweep over occupied France, fine and crisp with scattered cloud sufficient to give cover without reducing visibility. Victor Beamish had been seen away from Kenley to meet and cover a returning Spitfire formation made up of three squadrons that had been attacking ground-installations near Calais. The mêlée that resulted when the formations met found a weaving mass of fighters with the Nazi machines providing an echo of the Channel operation of six weeks before, due to the presence of no less than fifty Focke-Wulf 190s, the relatively new design that had distinguished itself over the battle-cruisers, although there were some of the familiar Me 109s.

Behind the Group-Captain flew a New Zealander, Flight-Lieutenant Reg Grant. As the Spitfires dived into the fight, so sharply that the pilots had to fight to keep their vision clear as the force drained the sight from their eyes, one of the Focke-Wulfs suddenly put in an appearance on the tail of the leader. Warning calls over the radio brought no response, and the pilot flying as No 2 took up the cry as well. A moment later the Nazi flashed into Grant's reflector sight, but even as the tracer from his guns began punching an ugly hole in its port wing, fire from the same aircraft could be seen ripping into the Group-Captain's Spitfire.

A moment more and the enemy was screaming down with an aileron torn away; Victor Beamish seemed to be turning for home. Grant was now behind to protect his leader's tail and almost immediately proved his usefulness when a Messerschmitt appeared as if from nowhere, seemingly intent on finishing off the first machine, but before he could get the Kenley fighter within range, the New Zealander put in a well-placed burst of cannon fire that blew up the Messerschmitt in a ball of red-centred orange flame.

By now the fight was some 5 miles from the French coast and at 13,000 feet, with the Group-Captain flying straight and level, making good speed. In front loomed one of those scattered small banks of cloud that had made the day so ideal for the mission. The two Spitfires entered this, with the leader a little ahead. Emerging, Grant saw a lone fighter below. He closed on it and looked for a wave from his Group-Captain. None came. Puzzled, he let his gaze slip back for the reassuring letters, FV B. His senses tightened as he saw they were not there. He had formated on another Spitfire, and that of his leader had vanished from the sky in the brief moments the two were in the cloud.

The last of the principal actors in the saga of 'Operation Fuller' or 'Cerberus' had disappeared, seemingly without trace, and was never seen or heard of again.

Back at the little Surrey fighter station where he had become a familiar sight taking exercise on the perimeter track soon after six each morning, in the manner of the sportsman he still was at heart, men gathered in little groups and spoke in low tones of the wintry day when Group-Captain Beamish DSO and Bar, DFC, AFC, had secured his place in history, when the lone hunt had found him and Wing-Commander Boyd twisting and turning to evade the murderous fire from the Nazi flotilla they had blundered upon. Sergeant Jessop had sadly inked in the margin of a cutting about his former Station-Commander his date of death, "28.3.42", adding later "about 5 p.m.".

Index